ANTONY AND CLEOPATRA

THEORY IN PRACTICE SERIES

General Editor: Nigel Wood, School of English, University of Birmingham

Associate Editors: Tony Davies and Barbara Rasmussen, University of Birmingham

Titles:

ANTONY AND # CLEOPATRA

EDITED BY
NIGEL WOOD

OPEN UNIVERSITY PRESS
BUCKINGHAM · PHILADELPHIA

Open University Press
Celtic Court
22 Ballmoor
Buckingham
MK18 1XW

and
1900 Frost Road, Suite 101
Bristol, PA 19007, USA

First Published 1996

A catalogue record of this book is available from the British Library

ISBN 0 335 15692 4 (pb)

Library of Congress Cataloging-in-Publication Data

Antony and Cleopatra / edited by Nigel Wood; Barbara J. Baines . . .
[et al.].
    p. cm. — (Theory in practice series)
Includes bibliographical references and index.
ISBN 0-335-15692-4
    1. Shakespeare, William, 1564–1616. Antony and Cleopatra.
2. Cleopatra, Queen of Egypt, d. 30 B.C. — In literature. 3. Antonius,
Marcus, 83?–30 B.C. — In literature. 4. Generals in literature.
5. Queens in literature. 6. Egypt — In literature. 7. Rome — In literature.
8. Tragedy. I. Wood, Nigel, 1953– . II. Baines, Barbara J. (Barbara
Joan) III. Series.
PR2802.A78 1996
822.3'3 — dc20   95–31560 CIP

Typeset by Colset Pte. Ltd, Singapore
Printed in Great Britain by St Edmundsbury Press,
Bury St Edmunds, Suffolk

For Chris, Irene, Adam and Laura

Contents

The Editor and Contributors

BARBARA J. BAINES is a professor of English literature at North Carolina State University in Raleigh, where she regularly teaches courses in Shakespeare at graduate and undergraduate levels. Her publications include numerous articles on Shakespeare and on other Renaissance dramatists and a book on Thomas Heywood. She is currently working on a study of sexuality and suicide in Renaissance drama.

DYMPNA CALLAGHAN is associate professor in the Department of English and Textual Studies at Syracuse University. She is author of *Woman and Gender In Renaissance Tragedy* (1989) and co-author of *The Weyward Sisters: Shakespeare and Feminist Politics* (1994).

MARY HAMER is the author of *Signs of Cleopatra: History, Politics, Representation* (1993) and of *Writing by Numbers: Trollope's Serial Fiction* (1987). She has also edited two of Trollope's Irish novels, *Castle Richmond* and *The Landleaguers*, and published articles on a range of subjects including the nineteenth-century mapping of Ireland.

ROBERT WILCHER is senior lecturer in English at the University of Birmingham. Publications include *Andrew Marvell* (British and Irish Authors series, 1985), *Andrew Marvell: Selected Poetry and Prose* (1986), *Understanding Arnold Wesker* (1991), a chapter on the radio plays in *Beckett's Later Fiction and Drama: Texts for Company* edited by

James Acheson and Kateryna Arthur (1987), and articles in various periodicals on Milton, Marvell, Vaughan, *Eikon Basilike*, Shakespeare, and modern drama. A forthcoming article on Quarles is part of a larger project on Royalist writing of the mid-seventeenth century.

NIGEL WOOD is senior lecturer in English at the University of Birmingham. He is the author of a study of Jonathan Swift, has edited essays on John Gay and a selection of Frances Burney's journals and letters. As general editor of the *Theory in Practice* series he has edited, or co-edited, seven volumes, the most recent being those on *The Tempest* and *Henry IV, Parts One and Two* (both 1995).

Editors' Preface

The object of this series is to help bridge the divide between the understanding of theory and the interpretation of individual texts. Students are therefore introduced to theory in practice: Although contemporary critical theory is now taught in many colleges and universities, it is often separated from the day-to-day consideration of literary texts that is the staple ingredient of most tuition in English. A thorough dialogue between theoretical and literary texts is thus avoided.

Each of these specially commissioned volumes of essays seeks by contrast to involve students of literature in the questions and debates that emerge when a variety of theoretical perspectives are brought to bear on a selection of 'canonical' literary texts. Contributors were not asked to provide a comprehensive survey of the arguments involved in a particular theoretical position, but rather to discuss in detail the implications for interpretation found in particular essays or studies, and then, taking these into account, to offer a reading of the literary text.

This rubric was designed to avoid two major difficulties which commonly arise in the interaction between literary and theoretical texts: the temptation to treat a theory as a bloc of formulaic rules that could be brought to bear on any text with roughly predictable results; and the circular argument that texts are constructed as such merely by the theoretical perspective from which we choose to regard them. The former usually leads to studies that are really just footnotes to the adopted theorists, whereas the latter is effortlessly self-fulfilling.

It would be disingenuous to claim that our interests in the teaching of theory were somehow neutral and not open to debate. The idea for this series arose from the teaching of theory in relation to specific texts. It is inevitable, however, that the practice of theory poses significant questions as to just what 'texts' might be and where the dividing lines between text and context may be drawn. Our hope is that this series will provide a forum for debate on just such issues as these which are continually posed when students of literature try to engage with theory in practice.

Tony Davies
Barbara Rasmussen
Nigel Wood

Preface

I have been helped in a variety of ways by the forbearance of good friends during the preparation of this volume: Sharon Ouditt and Martin Stannard with wine and sympathy, Carol Horsburgh with neighbourly understanding and practical help at the crucial time. It is also time to record my thanks to Richard Leigh, the copy-editor for the series, whose advice and judgement have been invariably sound and intelligent and whose enthusiasm for the project went well beyond the call of mere duty.

As usual, the contributors have been cooperative, and often helped with diplomatic and thoughtful suggestions.

Nigel Wood

How to Use
this Book

Each of these essays is composed of a theoretical and a practical element. Contributors were asked to identify the main features of their perspective on the text (exemplified by a single theoretical essay or book) and then to illustrate their own attempts to put this into practice.

We realize that many readers new to recent theory will find its specific vocabulary and leading concepts strange and difficult to relate to current critical traditions in most English courses.

The format of this book has been designed to help if this is your situation, and we would advise the following:

(i)   Before reading the essays, glance at the editor's introduction where the literary text's critical history is discussed, and

(ii) also at the prefatory information immediately before the essays, where the editor attempts to supply a context for the adopted theoretical position.

(iii) If you would like to develop your reading in any of these areas, turn to the annotated further reading section at the end of the volume, where you will find brief descriptions of those texts that each contributor has considered of more advanced interest. There are also full citations of the texts to which the contributors have referred in the references. It is also possible that more local information will be contained in notes to the essays.

(iv) The contributors have often regarded the chosen theoretical texts as points of departure and it is also in the nature of theoretical discussion to apply and test ideas on a variety of texts. Turn, therefore, to question and answer sections that follow each essay which are designed to allow contributors to comment and expand on their views in more general terms.

A Note on
the Texts Used

Quotations from *Antony and Cleopatra* are from the Oxford University Press edition by Michael Neill (Oxford, 1994). Unlike Neill, however, I have not adopted his thoroughly modernized *Anthony*, preferring more classical associations. On the other hand, Neill's arguments for his procedures on proper names are logical and stand up to close textual scrutiny (see his 'Introduction', pp. 131–5). In addition, the following Shakespeare editions have been consulted:

As You Like It	ed. Alan Brissenden (Oxford, 1993)
The Comedy of Errors	ed. T. S. Dorsch (Cambridge, 1988)
Coriolanus	ed. R.B. Parker (Oxford, 1994)
Hamlet	ed. G.R. Hibbard (Oxford, 1987)
Julius Caesar	ed. Marvin Spevack (Cambridge, 1988)
The Merchant of Venice	ed. Jay L. Halio (Oxford, 1994)
A Midsummer Night's Dream	ed. R.A. Foakes (Cambridge, 1984)
Much Ado About Nothing	ed. Sheldon P. Zitner (Oxford, 1994)
Troilus and Cressida	ed. Kenneth Muir (Oxford, 1982)
The Winter's Tale	ed. J.H.P. Pafford (London, 1963)

Introduction

NIGEL WOOD

For all its epic scope, *Antony and Cleopatra* is often found wanting in its
Aristotelian action. This is not merely a pedantic cavil at some irregular
masterpiece. As Robert Wilcher argues (in this volume, pp.
95–104)
generic features are often particularly difficult to judge as their match
with some notional entity might actually prejudice our attempts to
regard them as part of an original undertaking. The need to fit the play
into some five-act structure entails a desperate attempt to find some
immanent form for the potentially episodic Acts III and IV. The Folio
text showed no act divisions, which were probably first formulated for
the play by Nicholas Rowe in his 1709 edition, together with geographical locations. Consequently, there has been an uncomfortable critical
realization that we no longer share the conventions that Shakespeare
both deployed and perhaps parodied in the play. For Samuel Johnson in
1765 the breathless succession of scenes derived from Shakespeare's great
desire to describe history, not forge art, and it resulted in an action where
there was no 'art of connection or care of disposition'. At the same time,
there was a 'continual hurry' where the 'curiosity' was always kept
'busy', and the 'passions always interested' (Johnson 1986: 297–8): intellect versus passion – a very suitable binary opposition for a commentary
on the play, and note how it emerges as an Alexandrian experience.[1]

For Aristotle, the abiding distinction that helps characterize
successful art is that between Art and History. In his Chapter IX of
the *Poetics*, probability (*eikos*) and necessity (*ananke*) are taken to be
constituent qualities in Art, but not History:

> it is not the function of the poet to narrate events that have actually happened, but rather, events such as might occur and have the capability of occurring in accordance with the laws of probability and necessity . . . poetry is more concerned with the universal, and history more with the individual.
>
> (Aristotle 1968: 16–17)[2]

The connective links between narrative items actually bear on views of human free will. Necessary relations, as Aristotle remarks both in the *Nicomachean Ethics* (1139a) and the *Rhetoric* (1356b–57a) bear on non-human affairs, whose sphere of causation is the probable. Aristotle regards art in this further distinction as affording a necessary doubt about the power of events to structure the human sphere. Nature can operate with a direct relation between cause and effect, but Art can only advance propositions, not laws. O.B. Hardison, Jnr's helpful commentary on Chapter IX puts this concisely:

> The arrival of the messenger in *Oedipus* is the immediate cause for the blinding episode, but what is the cause of the messenger's arrival at just the right moment? Again, in . . . *Henry IV, Part I*, the scenes alternate between the revels of Hal, Falstaff, and company in the Boar's Head Tavern and scenes in the 'rebel camp' featuring Hotspur and his cohorts. In what sense does a scene in the Boar's Head Tavern 'cause' a scene at the rebel camp? The answer is plainly, in no sense; yet *Henry IV* is a tightly constructed and effective play.
>
> (Aristotle 1968: 153–4)

Artistic unity, therefore, always requires some sleight of hand, and, unlike the typical operations of natural laws, Aristotelian universals imply no neoclassical certainties. As Stephen Halliwell notes, the pursuit of verisimilitude 'might be satisfied precisely by vividness of particulars', as long as they eventually provide a bridge to essential forms of the 'real' ('Aristotle's Poetics', in Kennedy 1989: 155). For Sir Philip Sidney, in his *Apology for Poetry* (1595), Aristotle propounded the idea that the goal was not knowing, but doing, not *gnosis* but *praxis* (Sidney 1973: 112).

This oscillation between *praxis* and the frustrated sense of almost but not quite knowing should not be confused with more hardened later formulations of the unities. Artistic integrity allows surface formal variety, and, as Emrys Jones perceived in *Antony and Cleopatra*, the play pursues two contrary impulses. The first details Antony's separation from Caesar; the second, commencing in Act III, scene vii, pursues both Antony and Cleopatra to their death, 'an arrangement which reflects the historical process' (Jones 1971: 230). Both movements end with Caesar as the centre of focus; he advises Octavia at the end of Act III, scene vi, to 'let determined things to destiny/Hold unbewailed their way' (III.vi.85–6), as if he held the reins of destiny. He is there at the end voicing a less than fulsome elegy for the lovers:

> No grave upon the earth shall clip in it
> A pair so famous. High events as these
> Strike those that make them; and their story is
> No less in pity than his glory which
> Brought them to be lamented. Our army shall
> In solemn show attend this funeral –
> And then to Rome. Come, Dolabella, see
> High order in this great solemnity.
>
> (V.ii.357–64)

The pair are merely 'famous' (notorious?), and just who *has* made the 'high events' in which they have figured? Our pity should be in due proportion to our admiration for the 'glory' of their puppet-master, Octavius Caesar. For all Cleopatra's determination 'To fool [the Romans'] preparation' and 'conquer/Their most absurd intents' (V.ii.225–6), she and Antony will still shore up 'high order' and 'great solemnity' in the closing tableau. Octavius appropriates as he apparently celebrates, and there was nothing new in this. Consider the split commemoration of Brutus in *Julius Caesar*: Antony remembers 'the noblest Roman of them all', stressing his example in promoting a 'general honest thought/And common good to all', but Octavius caps this altruism with the egoistic desire to have the bones lie as a trophy in his tent before the provision of a *soldier's* funeral, 'ordered honourably'. We might read back at the comment that the victorious army should 'use' him 'According to his virtue' (V.v.68–79), as profoundly ambiguous, for when has this official Roman ideology had room for Brutus's conception of virtue? Four lines are spared for the dead, and Octavius is 'away/To part the glories of this happy day' (V.v.80–1).[3]

Even given the practical consideration that it would be a resonant end to the theatrical action to conclude it with a sonorous set-piece, one might wonder whether such a martial afflatus is in keeping with the Alexandrian or Republican sentiments that supply the significant 'other' to Roman imperialism – nor is this an isolated example. When Coriolanus is borne off the stage he is left to the mercies of those who remember that he 'hath widowed and unchilded many a one,/Which to this hour bewail the injury' (*Coriolanus*, V.vi.152–3). Just as four captains bear Hamlet off the stage, four are provided for Coriolanus, but as Parker (1994: 115) points out, these pall-bearers are likely to be the very conspirators who have just done him down. Hamlet, too, is given the soldier's burial at which the preceding action rarely hints. The still and moving dialogue between Horatio and Hamlet can be rudely interrupted by the 'warlike noise' of Fortinbras's approach (*Hamlet*, V.ii.302). Horatio hopes for 'flights of angels' to 'sing' him 'to his rest', and he well may enquire, 'Why does the drum come hither?' (V.ii.313–14), yet what the audience actually sees is Hamlet accommodated to a warrior's image, where 'The soldiers' music and the rites of war' end up speaking 'loudly for him' (V.ii.352–3). The Folio has a 'Peale of Ordenance . . . shot off' as the closing gesture of the action.

It is unlikely that Cleopatra is allowed to be interred in her own monument. Octavius chooses her resting-place, although we could choose to imagine her spirit already by the Cydnus with Antony. Miola (1983: 163) senses that the monument 'finally occupies the center of our interests and sympathies, and the entering Romans appear as impious invaders', yet one could just as easily see them as successfully bearing her from her sacred place. Jones (1971: 230) regards Caesar's closing threnody as uttered by the 'detached, yet all-comprehending voice of the historian, or rather the historical poet'. The alternatives offered by Jones are not evidence of indecisiveness, but, on the contrary, point to the extra-textual knowledge which an audience could bring to the narrative. Plutarch reminded his readers that 'it was predestined that the government of all the world should fall into Octavius Caesars handes' (Bullough 1957–75, 5: 292), and there is a similar dramatic irony about the Volscians' success at the close of *Coriolanus*, which was but a prelude to four and a half centuries of Roman hegemony, Aufidius's death and their extirpation.

History cannot account for the particular relationship that audiences might form with the narrated events of a drama, but it is a tacit ingredient in the poetic symbols formed out of its raw data. Its 'Necessity' overrides the 'Probability' on which Art relies, but only off-stage, as a trace. We ought perhaps to return to the series of projected oppositions between passion and order illustrated by Johnson's appreciation of the breathlessness of the play's construction. History is a succession of rapid events that appear not to represent present or retrospectively maufactured order, yet the audience is reminded at cardinal moments that Caesar is favoured by Historical necessity, not Antony or Cleopatra.[4]

The question as to whether the play possesses an acceptable degree of unity is often posed as an aesthetic preference; the play lacks a heterocosmic unity and so is not sufficiently hived off from anarchic reality. That preference is, however, predicated on assumptions that are not necessarily always the reaction of some transhistorical audience. What is dramatic about the handling of certain narratives can perish, as responses to drama need not only consult one's memories of previous artistic occasions, other 'probabilities'. In Jonathan Dollimore's influential account of *Radical Tragedy* (1984), the play's dramatic power is not demonstrated by recourse to notions of artistic effect that emerge from some unhistorical realm. Shakespeare may be recalling a time long the province of history books, but why write of such matters then? Doubtless, Sir Thomas North's translation of Plutarch's *Lives of the Noble Greeks and Romans* (1579) opened up certain topics of interest, and Shakespeare undoubtedly used the translation as a source, but Dollimore focuses on the way that early Jacobean concerns were mediated through this classical filter, in particular the decline in 'martial ideology' and the 'erasure of older notions of honour and *virtus*' (Dollimore 1984: 204). Antony comes to recognize the consequences of relinquishing the Roman power structure that permeated the way he constructed his own self-image: 'the heroic *virtus* which he wants to reaffirm in and through Cleopatra is in fact almost entirely a function of the power structure which he, again ambivalently, is prepared to sacrifice for her' (Dollimore 1984: 217). This double bind mitigates any full claim the character may have for a traditional tragic status.

What is analysed in the depiction of Antony's desire is the dissolution of a Roman personality. At the same time as Antony notes ever-changing cloud formations in Act IV, scene xv, he feels intimations of mortality. In a scene heavy with figurative excess, the dialogue with the aptly named Eros depicts Antony on the threshold of a full realization of just what Alexandrian values might mean for a Roman:

ANTHONY: Eros, thou yet behold'st me?
EROS: Ay, noble lord.
ANTHONY: Sometime we see a cloud that's dragonish,
   A vapour sometime like a bear or lion,
   A towered citadel, a pendant rock,
   A forked mountain, or blue promontory
   With trees upon't that nod unto the world
   And mock our eyes with air. Thou hast seen these signs –
   They are black vesper's pageants.

                                                         (IV.xv.1–8)

Towered citadels and forked mountains turn out to be vapour and signs. Moreover, Antony understands them as harbingers either of the evening of life, or at least its decline. The main point seems to consist in the reflection (actual or symbolic) that all there might be is 'signs' and 'pageants'. 'Thought' decodes the shape into its actual constituent elements: as 'indistinct/As water is in water' (IV.xv.10–11), yet the imaginative eye is content to take the private association as reality enough. The merely corporeal perspective may trace no change in Antony, yet he is no exception to the law of clouds: 'here I am Anthony,/Yet cannot hold this visible shape' (IV.xv.13–14). When Mardian enters with the comfortless lie that Cleopatra is dead, Antony immediately bemoans the loss of the phallic and separatist potency on which, hitherto, his personal myth had been based: 'O, thy vile lady,/She has robbed me of my sword!' (IV.xv.22–3). Mardian's defence of his mistress suggests an alternative to aggressive selfhood, claiming that her love created identity not egoistic definition, as 'her fortunes mingled/With [his] entirely' (IV.xv.24–5). Eros then helps Antony disarm, an enactment of what the rhetorical signs had in any case already promoted. His armour had protected him but had also kept more than his body intact. Once off, Antony fears that his heart may have no carapace to check its flow, an ironic return to Philo's opening figure of his 'captain's heart' transformed into a disturber of air, 'the bellows and the fan/To cool a gypsy's lust' (I.i.9–10). 'No more a soldier. Bruisèd pieces, go' (IV.xv.42), he exclaims, and there is an instinctive overriding of the most obvious referent (his battered armour) by the possibility that they at the same time could be the fractured shards of his former self.

But is it a *former* self, or *any* self? There are at least two ways of comprehending answers to this query. The first locates Cleopatra's influence as a positive one, but in a mode that the overt text cannot grasp and decode for the audience in signs that admit of unequivocal or publically available interpretation (that is, it has to be assembled by visiting a modern preoccupation on to a Renaissance one). The second regards the text as marked by its inherited ideological patterns, but which also marks the satiric withdrawal from an easy assent to its narrative or stereotyped appeal ('*Virtus* under Erasure' in Dollimore 1984, 204–17). Satiric irony's potency lies in the fact that it need not come up with a viable alternative. By driving a wedge between an accepted understanding and a wider world of possible significance (that puts normality in its place), parody or situational irony points to flaws in an apparently stable consensus.

Cleopatra VII is historically significant as a temporal ruler as well as a powerful queen. According to the Alexandrian version recounted by Hughes-Hallett (1990: 95–143) and Hamer (1993: 5–23), she was philanthropic and learned. More glaring, however, is the silence in Shakespeare's play about North/Plutarch's praise of her accomplishments:

> so sweete was her companie and conversacion, that a man could not possiblie but be taken. And besides her beawtie, the good grace she had to talke and discourse, her curteous nature that tempered her words and dedes, was a spurre that pricked to the quick. Furthermore, besides all these, her voyce and words were marvelous pleasant: for her tongue was an instrument of musicke to divers sports and pastimes, the which she easely turned to any language that pleased her.
>
> (Bullough 1957–75, 5: 275)

Here is a decorous woman, yet one who delighted in infinite variety, lacking the goal-centred blinkers of the drive to power. This is not the whole story. The civil war between her and her brother Ptolemy XIII was only decided after she had seduced Julius Caesar to side with her. This was not, however, the only irritant to Roman good form. Cleopatra was a *visible* woman (on coins and at Alexandrian public spectacles) at a time when the only publically recognized women in Rome were regarded as sexually outrageous (see Hamer 1993: 20–21). As Hughes-Hallett (1990:75–6) makes plain, her power over Julius Caesar became a parable of male impotence, which scrambled distinct gender roles. For Mary Hamer and Barbara Baines (this volume, pp. 72–88, 24–37) this mix of sexual threat and un-Roman desire, delivered by Octavian propaganda, needs to be accounted for in un-Roman terms so that the new accents of Alexandrian freedoms can be heard. Similarly, Dympna Callaghan's exploration of a 'Subaltern' perspective alerts criticism to the play's elements of parody and textual play.

Antony and Cleopatra is a Jacobean document, and that does not necessarily entail a departure from the previous point. As H. Neville Davies (and others) have pointed out (Davies 1985; Morris 1969; Reinhart 1972), the idea that the English were living on after what many still regarded as a stirring chapter in the national heritage made particularly resonant lines such as Cleopatra's

> the odds is gone,
> And there is nothing left remarkable
> Beneath the visiting moon.
>
> (IV.xvi.68–70)

As Davies (1985: 124) phrases it, 'the deprivation is devastating, for without Cleopatra's voice we seem even to lack a speaker able to record the loss'. *Was* there a widespread cultural malaise? In 1604, as Dollimore (1984: 169–74) and Yachnin (1993) have pointed out, there was a possible period of trial for absolutist theories of government. Yachnin reads Dolabella's role as vital. Is he swayed by Cleopatra or does he remain loyal to Caesar? His attempts at interruption in Act V, scene ii, need careful handling in production. He feels a grief at Cleopatra's plight 'that smites/[His] very heart at root' (V.ii.104–5), and as he is charged with the funeral arrangements, he could be part of a test of loyalty, an ingredient of an already complex set of closing symbols.

Do Antony and Cleopatra escape the inexorable fate of a historically favoured Caesar? Janet Adelman's optimistic view, one that embraces the uncertainty principle in a positive spirit, finds the varying perspectives we entertain about the work as necessary in comprehending its emotional structure. A casualty of this is its standing as tragedy, where the 'comic perspective' destroys the necessary concentration of mood that tragedy requires (Adelman 1973: 44–52). More stands to be lost, however, than a tragedy from the canon. Tragedy engrosses us with its depiction of individual destiny. We see this focus blurred and dissipated within the play, just as it appeared to the new thought of Jacobean culture[5] a victory of necessity over artistic and other ordering.

CHAPTER 1

Girard's Doubles and *Antony and Cleopatra*

BARBARA J. BAINES

[Aristotle's theory of imitation, or mimesis, is susceptible to two opposed interpretations. The more common understanding is that we imitate because it is a natural human attribute. In the *Poetics*, this power is the basic motive for poetry: 'The process of imitation is natural to mankind from childhood on: Man is differentiated from other animals because he is the most imitative of them, and he learns his first lessons through imitation, and we observe that all men find pleasure in imitations' (Aristotle 1968: 7). This educative function brings pleasure, which is increased when we note the natural original in the artful copy. This persists even when the representation is of ugliness or meanness that otherwise would be painful: we can still admire the care taken to render it for the artistic occasion. Realism, carefully deployed, is thus the corner-stone of mimesis, where the signified is logically prior to the signifier, and can therefore provide a guarantee of its representative function, which is not limited to a photographic literalism, but has the power to sum up and define.

For René Girard, this move to represent need not be explained merely by relating it to some invariable human impulse. To define is to appropriate, and so domesticate, perhaps, but it can also involve a sublimation of rivalry and competition. This is the common reflection of his first studies of the mimetic drive: his *Mensonge, romantique et verité romanesque* (1961; trans. as *Deceit, Desire and the Novel* (Girard 1965)). To imitate might indicate the forms of appropriative desire. In *La Violence et le sacré* (1972; trans. as *Violence and the Sacred* (Girard 1977a)), Girard reviews Greek tragedy and Freudian psychoanalysis as well as Shakespeare's plays as examples of competitive mimesis, and even claims that modern developed cultures might manifest 'runaway' mimetic desire in their fictions because they lack the checks on aberrant and asocial behaviour to be observed in 'primitive' cultures. Violence simmers just under the surface of modern manners and can erupt at the point where an agreed or recognized 'sacred' regulation of social life breaks down. Often, to keep the pattern intact, or at least in view, there has to be the sacrifice of some substitute figure, who may not be directly responsible for the initial disorder. A crisis occurs when the delicate balance of the sacrificial act, its fine gradations and distinctions, is affected (see Girard 1977a: 39–67). This usually emerges when the sacred qualities invested in the sacrifical victim are diluted by either too near a similarity between him and the actual forces he represents or too great a divorce between them in reference or significance:

> A single principle is at work in primitive religion and classical tragedy alike, a principle implicit but fundamental. Order, peace, and fecundity depend on cultural distinctions; it is not these distinctions but the loss of them that gives birth to fierce rivalries and sets members of the same family or social group at one another's throats.
>
> (Girard 1977a: 49)

Too much agreement carries in its wake a fear of a loss of individuality, and a renewed search for a necessary, 'original' division to underpin accepted definitions and 'essence'. The sacred can therefore only be upheld by violence, and this becomes particularly marked in the example of 'enemy twins' (Girard 1977a: 56–64), brothers too near the same throne. One intends violence in order to restore a sense of self and scapegoating is the result. The appearance of twins suggests duplication, not distinction, and this prompts an internecine struggle. In *The Comedy of Errors*, for example, Shakespeare exploits this web of misunderstanding surrounding two sets of identical twins, Antipholus and Dromio, from both Ephesus and Syracuse. There is an obvious comic confusion here, but both these cities are sufficiently distinct for the desperate farce to avoid too much uncomfortable scapegoating. *The Winter's Tale*, however, might start with Leontes and Polixenes as 'twinn'd lambs that did frisk i' th' sun' (I.ii.67), but the threat of the latter usurping the married prerogative of the former brings ungovernable rage and the death of the King's son, Mamillius. Together with the (apparent) death of Hermione, Sicilian order is restored, and distinction restored.

It is imperative to note that Girard envisages these literary-critical reflections as involving more than just a method of textual understanding. The darker side to mimetic desire is a social pattern:

> The historical mutilation of mimesis, the supression of its conflictual dimension, was no mere oversight, no fortuitous 'error'. Real awareness of mimetic desire threatens the flattering delusion we entertain not only about ourselves as individuals but also about the nature and origin of that collective self we call our society. If mimesis, like all primitive gods, has two 'sides', one that disrupts the com-

munity and another one that holds it together, how do the two sides relate to each other?

(Girard 1978b: xii)

As Barbara Baines points out (p. 15), Shakespeare's understanding of 'Degree' could be said to share this determination to escape undifferentiated existence.

Most myths embrace a narrative of how a society might pursue a (re-)constructive principle of social integration after the threat to the sacred is dispersed by expiation and sacrifice. Girard moves to the more positive thesis that every myth helps a community survive these anarchic forces deep within its self. Latterly, he has turned to the Christian gospel for this cultural power (see his *Des Choses cachées depuis la fondation du monde* (*Things Hidden since the Foundation of the World* of 1977; Girard 1977b), and also his *Le Bouc emissaire The Scapegoat* of 1982; Girard 1986).

In more aesthetic matters, Girard's careful questioning of our sustaining fictions about ourselves could equally well apply to 'normal' interpretations of how literary texts reflect social reality, that is, how often we turn a blind eye to potentially destructive or 'deconstructive' readings. Jacques Derrida notes that the scapegoat or *pharmakos* is always chosen from within the *polis*, not from the ranks of the enemy. This mythical medicine or *pharmakon* needs to be a replenishing of one's integrity from within, a reminder that the identification of internal/external relations is a necessary cultural reflex, but a distinction not otherwise discernible:

> The ceremony of the *pharmakos* is thus played out on the boundary line between the inside and outside, which it has as its function to trace and retrace repeatedly. *Intra muros/extra muros*. Origin of difference and division, the *pharmakos* represents evil both introjected and projected.

(Derrida 1982: 133)

Which is why Shylock in *The Merchant of Venice* resembles the gentiles so much.]

NIGEL WOOD

I

I first became interested in René Girard when I heard him give a paper some years ago at Duke University on *The Merchant of Venice*. Like most readers, I had always been troubled by the anti-Semitism within and of this play and was very conscious of the binary oppositions constructed and subtly deconstructed within the play. And like many readers, I had always been ill at ease with the self-righteous, somewhat hypocritical and more than somewhat blind nature of the

Christian characters with whom the play seems to invite sympathy. What I had not seen, and what Girard's paper obliged me to see, is the extent to which the chief antagonists, Antonio and Shylock, are doubles. The effect of this paper was to make me conscious of how prevailing this kinship or similarity between antagonists is throughout the Shakespeare canon.

The value of Girard's theoretically grounded reading of Shakespeare for me lies in its broad applicability. No other critic has, in my opinion, defined so convincingly the playwright's profound insight concerning the driving force in human nature. The tendency of other critics is to focus somewhat narrowly on a genre: tragedy, comedy, 'problem' plays, or romances. What Girard, in contrast, has done is to find the common denominator, tracing its variations and permutations, and thus to offer a holistic view of Shakespeare's plays. His latest work, *A Theater of Envy* (Girard 1991), is the record of this endeavour. For Girard, the unifying and governing insight of all of Shakespeare's plays pertains to mimetic desire. I was surprised to discover that *Antony and Cleopatra* is not among the many plays that Girard has chosen to analyse in his latest book or in previously written essays. In fact, I have found only a few very brief references to this play in all of Girard's works. He explains that he selected for discussion those plays which most explicitly serve his purposes and which generally are the first (or early) within the genre to develop a particular 'mimetic configuration' (Girard 1991: 7). At the end of this essay, I will return to the question of why Girard might have omitted *Antony and Cleopatra* from his discussion of Shakespeare's plays, despite the fact that this play is the dramatization *par excellence* of mimetic rivalry. First, let me begin with an account of Girard's theory in which mimetic rivalry is of paramount importance.

Throughout his long and highly influential career, René Girard has persistently articulated a theory of mimesis that accounts for human conflict. To Girard, mimesis is as basic to the human condition as the drives are to Freud. In fact, Girard has at least on one occasion referred to 'an increased mimetic drive corresponding to the enlarged human brain' (Girard 1978a: 33). Without the desire to imitate, there would be no forms of representation and no human community. What the subject imitates is the desire of an 'other'. Girard identifies this 'other' as the model or the mediator of desire and consequently the subject's rival. Mimetic desire generally results in mimetic rivalry that escalates into a crisis of violence that can be resolved only through 'unanimous victimage'. To this theory of mimesis in which desire, rivalry, and violence are inextricably connected, the double business of Girard's study of literature and of anthropology is bound; for this theory accounts for conflict in ethnological texts of myth and ritual as well as in literary text. The Introduction to 'To Double Business Bound': Essays on Literature, Mimesis, and Anthropology (Girard 1978b) and the essay 'Lévi-Strauss, Frye, Derrida and Shakespearean Criticism' (Girard 1973) provide Girard's concise explanation of his theory of mimetic desire and its relevance to literature and will therefore be the primary texts for the following summary and discussion.

Although throughout the history of Western civilization mimesis, or imitation, has been a primary concern of numerous disciplines, its darker dimension has been ignored since Plato (and, according to Girard, inadequately comprehended by him) in the pursuit of its more positive aesthetic and educational aspects, described by Aristotle. According to Aristotle, imitation is a natural instinct, and art is always an imitation, or perhaps more accurately, a representation of action – action being best understood as a movement of the human spirit or will (see Fergusson 1961). The pleasure of imitation resides in the viewer's or listener's recognition of that which is familiar in the representation. What we, under the influence of Aristotle, have failed to see, according to Girard, is the extent to which the subject of imitation is desire, which is itself mimetic, and that the aim of mimetic desire is appropriation. For Girard, this is the message, a quasi-theoretical message, inherent in certain literary texts universally recognized as 'great masterpieces'. These works are privileged because they are 'more mimetic' in the sense that 'they portray human relations and desire as mimetic', but they are also more mimetic in the traditional sense of their resemblance to the best of the ancient writers with whom they share the revelation of the mimetic nature of desire (Girard 1978b: ix). Girard suggests that we have resisted this insight into the mimetic nature of desire because it destroys 'the dearest of all our illusions, the intimate conviction that our desires are really our own, that they are truly original and spontaneous' (Girard 1978b: ix). The consequences of mimetic revelation extend, then, to the artist as well: the 'passage from mimetic reflection to mimetic revelation' results in 'the shattering of a mimetic reflection that complacently mirrors itself as pure originality and spontaneity' (Girard 1978b: x).

The disquieting aspect of Girard's theory of mimesis is not simply that the subject of mimesis is desire and that our desires are thus never really our own, but that mimetic desire results usually in mimetic rivalry and thus in a perpetual cycle of violence, reflected in the greatest literary texts, as well as in the ethnological texts of myth and ritual. Girard's understanding of mimetic rivalry and conflict derives from his study of literature, and to the great literary texts to which he urges us to turn if we are to understand and contend with the destructive as well as the beneficial effects of mimesis: 'We must unravel the paradoxical but logical network of mimetic entanglements spun by the great literary works' (Girard 1978b: x). We must, in short, see the delusion of autonomy and the misrecognition of antagonists whose conflicts derive both from what they have in common and from what they cannot share.

What certain literary texts reveal is the mediated nature of desire. Girard uses the terms 'external' and 'internal' to define two types of mediation. External mediation occurs when the spheres of the model and imitator are separated so that they cannot reach for the same object; thus differentiation can be preserved and the violence of rivalry avoided. When the mediation is external, the imitator frequently finds his model in books and legends. For example, Don Quixote's model is Amadis of Gaul; the models for Dante's Paola and Franscesca are Lancelot and Guinevere (Girard 1978b: 1–3). In the case of internal mediation (described in detail in the first chapter of *Deceit, Desire and the Novel* (Girard 1965) and concisely summarized in *Violence and the Sacred*) (Girard 1977a)), the subject's desire for an object is elicited by another's desire for the same object. This third presence is the rival whose desire the subject imitates. In other words, rivalry does not exist as a simple convergence of the desires of two subjects for the same object; rather, the desire of the subject for a particular object is generated by the desire of a rival for that object. The rival thus becomes the model, dictating to the subject not only matters of style and opinion but also the object of value. It is in this sense that desire itself is essentially mimetic and that the violent opposition of rivals is the signifier of ultimate desire. As Livingston (1992: 33–5) explains, Girard presupposes always that the model cannot function as such unless the imitator sees in the model qualities that elicit the imitator's esteem. Girard's recent analysis of Shakespeare's early and very perplexing comedy, *The Two Gentlemen of Verona* (Girard 1989; revised and included in Girard 1991: 8–20), is an excellent example of the 'practice' of Girard's theory of mimetic desire. Here the literary text seems virtually to generate the theory and thus illustrates perfectly Girard's conviction that certain literary texts are 'quasi-theoretical'. Valentine functions as the model for Proteus. When Valentine shows little admiration for Julia but idealizes Silvia, Proteus suddenly desires what the model desires. Proteus's desire for Silvia has nothing to do with her *per se*; his desire is grounded in, generated by, the desire of the model rival 'other' who is paradoxically his dearest friend and arch rival.

Although Girard established his reputation as a literary critic with his study of mimetic rivalry and triangulated desire in the novel (Girard 1965), the literary texts of greatest interest to him have consistently been the plays of Shakespeare. His most recent publication (Girard 1991) attests to this prevailing interest. In the 1978 *Diacritics* interview (Girard 1978a, reprinted in Girard 1978b), Girard accounts for his interest in Shakespeare as the author who most clearly and consistently reveals 'the hidden role of mimetic effects in human interaction' (Girard 1978a: 31). In his earlier essay in *Diacritics*, Girard (1973) makes clear the relevance of Shakespeare's plays to his theory of mimetic desire and rivalry. Part of an ongoing critique of structuralism and of Lévi-Strauss, this essay redefines the relationship between the undifferentiated and the differentiated in myth and ritual. Girard charges Lévi-Strauss with the failure to recognize the importance and function of the undifferentiated in myth and ritual. The literary structuralists, guilty according to Girard of the same obsession with differentiation, have no way of accounting for

> those writers, Shakespeare, for instance, who are obsessed with chaos, with the destruction of institutions and hierarchies, the reversal and obliteration of even sexual identities, with countless phenomena which amount, in other words, to a dissolving of differences.
>
> (Girard 1973: 34)

The modern assumption is that conflict arises out of difference; for the Greeks and for Shakespeare, however, 'the undifferentiated is closely associated with conflict' (Girard 1973: 34). Shakespeare's plays reveal the paradoxical relationship between difference and no difference. Fear of the ego-threatening undifferentiated, the horror of sameness, generates the conflicts through which antagonists attempt to assert difference. The conflicts then destroy the culturally constructed system designed to affirm difference, the system Shakespeare calls 'degree'.

Conflict not only is closely associated with the undifferentiated but is also the effect of desire. Because desire is mimetic, it 'focuses on some object already desired by the model and it necessarily brings disharmony and rivalry' (Girard 1973: 34). 'Hubris and mimetic rivalry are one' in the sense that they undermine the system of differences or degree – in Shakespeare's *Troilus and Cressida*, 'Degree with a capital D' (Girard 1973: 34). Paradoxically, mimetic rivalry

> is a quest for Difference that destroys whatever cultural reality there is to differences. Mimetic *hubris* is the equalizer *par excellence*, all the more powerful for going undetected. The end

result of the struggle is the stupid reciprocity of reprisals between undifferentiated antagonists . . .

(Girard 1973: 34)

In this paper as elsewhere, Girard identifies the antagonists within the pattern of mimetic rivalry and reciprocity as the 'doubles' of Shakespeare's tragedies and comedies. In the works of Shakespeare and of other writers who draw upon myth, the differences that are 'immutable and sacrosanct for the structuralists tend to dissolve into conflicts of *doubles*'. As difference dissolves into crisis in *Troilus and Cressida*, Shakespeare in this particular play becomes for Girard 'the greatest mythologist and interpreter of the Greeks ever' (Girard 1973: 34). Here Shakespeare makes explicit his understanding of the mediated nature of desire and rivalry. Politics and erotic desire, war and love, are governed by the same mimetic manipulation practised by Ulysses upon Achilles and Ajax and by Pandarus upon Troilus and Cressida. Shakespeare's debasement of Helen underscores the fact that she has no intrinsic value; rather she is valued by the Greeks simply because the Trojans determine to keep her and is valued by the Trojans because the Greeks would have her back. The desire of the 'other' constructs her as the object of appropriation. She is merely the context for a rivalry and conflict designed to assert difference or superiority but which ironically reveal the undifferentiated. Likewise, Troilus's desire for Cressida dies with his possession of her, only to be reborn through the mediation of 'the merry Greeks' (IV.iv.55) and specifically Diomed. As Girard explains: 'The mere possibility of losing Cressida to the Greeks makes her valuable again in the eyes of Troilus. If we do not attribute this wonderful metamorphosis of Troilus to *mimetic desire*, what shall it be?' (Girard 1991: 130).

Drawing on Girard's presentations at the English Department of the State University of New York at Buffalo, Joel Fineman provides additional insight into Girard's concept of mimetic rivalry and the perpetuating violence of 'doubles'. All myths are in some sense fratricide myths that reveal

the need to distinguish hero from villain, good from bad, in such a way that social value is itself corroborated. . . . Rival brothers . . . act out the myth of Difference, a story, always a story, by means of which societies ward off a catastrophe of order Girard labels as the crisis of 'No Difference' and that he defines as a loss of cultural distinctions so profound as to spell cultural suicide. The storied twins thus fight not so much to settle the differences between them (which, of course, can only barely exist, since equivalent brothers fight because they are the 'same'), but instead to establish through violence a definitive difference – victor-vanquished – by means of which they can be distinguished each from each.

(Fineman 1977: 428)

Myths capture the reality, the social artefact, of fratricide to represent it – one step removed, polarized and moralized – in terms of cultural order. Every society, then, reimagines itself within the myth of Difference (Fineman 1977: 428). In Girard's words, 'all human cultures have tried to convince themselves and others that the differences they set up are objective, stable, and permanent as the differences between natural species' (Girard 1973: 35). The problem with this effort is that what defines us specifically as human is a mutual dependence reflected in complex patterns of reciprocity that affect virtually every aspect of our lives. This reciprocity is the basic paradox of culture; for, although it is the essence of human interaction, it must be distorted or even suppressed; otherwise, mythical differences collapse and conflict emerges to reconstruct them. In Girard's (1973: 35) words: 'Myths and ritual tell us that differences are generated from that state of undifferentiation which we now identify with the reciprocal violence of the *doubles*'.

The survival of societies and cultures depends upon some mechanism that interrupts and reverses the reciprocal violence of mimetic rivalry, a mechanism that allows for reciprocal peace to substitute for the reciprocal violence. Girard accounts for this mechanism with his hypothesis of 'unanimous victimage', the subject of his book, *Violence and the Sacred* (1977a). Although Girard repeatedly cautions his readers that the complexities of unanimous victimage can be grasped only by reading *Violence and the Sacred*, he nevertheless explains the hypothesis in both the short essay 'Lévi-Strauss, Frye, Derrida, and Shakespearean Criticism' and in the introduction '*To Double Business Bound*', no doubt because this hypothesis is so integrally related to his theory of mimetic desire and rivalry. What follows here is first, an account of Girard's theory of unanimous victimage articulated in *Violence and the Sacred* and in his other works, and second, an account of Lacoue-Labarthe's (1978) response to Girard's theory.[1]

In *Violence and the Sacred*, Girard (1977a: 195) explains that Freud's *Totem and Taboo* was very important to his formulation of the concept of unanimous victimage. In this highly controversial work Freud provides 'clues that point to real collective murders as the origin and model of all ritual' (Girard 1978b: xii). Girard repeatedly insists upon real, generative events of violence and victimage which are reflected in myth and ritual. He contends that

[a]ll over the world, sacrificial immolation occurs at the climax and at the conclusion of mimetic free-for-alls that could be the reenactment of a spontaneously unanimous victimage. That victimage would terminate a truly disruptive mimetic crisis by reuniting the entire community against a single powerless antagonist

– the scapegoat. To the scapegoat is transferred all of the 'monstrous undifferentiation' resulting from the mimetic rivalry and sameness of the *doubles* (Girard 1973: 35). The scapegoat is a Janus figure, transfigured as the evil responsible for disorder and as the good whose death is the source of order: 'as a troublemaker and then a peacemaker, as an all-powerful manipulator of all human relations inside the community – in other words, a divinity' (Girard 1978b: xiv). Through the unanimous victimage of the scapegoat, reciprocal violence becomes reciprocal peace as Degree is restored. *Romeo and Juliet* provides an excellent illustration of this concept, for the Montagues and the Capulets are a perfect example of doubles. The rivalry between the two houses can be dispelled only by the sacrifice of the young lovers. 'Shakespeare knows that the doubles can be reconciled only at the expense of a common victim and that is sacrifice' (Girard 1973: 37).

Within the Shakespeare canon, Girard applies his theory of the scapegoat most effectively to Shylock in *The Merchant of Venice* and to Caesar in *Julius Caesar*. In the injustice of Shylock's story, readers generally recognize the scapegoat, but Girard stresses the need to recognize that the scapegoat may pertain to either the theme or the structure of the play or to both. When the author reveals that the scapegoat is unjustly condemned within a pattern of collective victimage, the scapegoat is a manifestation of theme. When, on the other hand, the author presents the character as justly condemned and punished, the scapegoat is an inherent part of the structure of the play. Shakespeare, in the latter case, would share in the anti-Semitism of his culture. Girard (1991: 248–9) perceptively contends that the key to our ambivalent response to this play is that the scapegoat is both theme and structure as Shakespeare both satirizes and participates in the victimage of Shylock. As doubles united in their mutual hatred, Antonio and Shylock share the identity of the scapegoat – a point made clear by Portia's question at the beginning of the trial, 'Which is the merchant here, and which the Jew?' (IV.i.171) and by Antonio's description of himself as 'a tainted wether of the flock,/Meetest for death' (IV.i.113–14).

For Girard *Julius Caesar* is the quintessential Shakespearian text illustrating the scapegoat mechanism. The action of the play occurs within a crisis of Degree as Republican Rome collapses to make way for the Roman Empire. Caesar's murder becomes 'the foundational violence' (Girard 1991: 201) for the Roman Empire, once Brutus and Caesar are united in death. In their union those who sided with either man are likewise united. As the leader of the conspiracy, Brutus perceives Caesar as the threat to order, to Degree, and thus as one who must be sacrificed for the good of Rome. Caesar, indeed, bears all the earmarks of the scapegoat: he is associated with deformity (the falling sickness, sterility and deafness) and with the monstrous or supernatural. His murder is consciously fashioned by Brutus as ritual sacrifice – 'a dish fit for the gods' (II.i.173). The sacrifice fails, however, to unite the crowd and instead precipitates the havoc of Philippi and thus a renewed cycle of violence.

Girard finds corroboration for his theory of victimage in the works of Northrop Frye and Jacques Derrida, specifically in their common concern with the Greek *pharmakos* or scapegoat. What particularly interests Girard in Frye's discussion of the *pharmakos* is his suggestion 'of the lynching mob as a generative force behind all myth and ritual' (Girard 1973: 36). Frye's suggestion, in fact, supports Girard's assertion that *Julius Caesar* is centred on collective violence and that 'the real subject is the violent crowd' (Girard 1991: 223). The mob, the undifferentiated, is human society looking for a *pharmakos*. The 'generative effect' of the *pharmakos* is somewhat clearer in Derrida's 'Plato's Pharmacy' (Derrida 1982: 61–156) than in Frye's *Anatomy of Criticism*. In Derrida's work the crucial word is *pharmakos* and its cognate, *pharmakon*,

which means both good and bad drug, medicine and poison. The drug can work either way, just like violence itself which is poison but may become its own cure through the single victim effect and the ritual reenactments of that effect.

(Girard 1973: 36)

In an effort to illuminate the relevance of Girard's theory of mimesis to Plato's understanding of psychology in *The Republic*, Lacoue-Labarthe (1978: 12) begins with an extremely important question: 'How does "psychology" contribute to mimetology?' For Plato the well-being of the state depends upon the subjugation of desire and the control of aggression; ' "Platonic psychology" is in fact a "psychology" of *desiring rivalry*, of the endless reciprocal hatred implied by the stuff of desire itself – precisely by its *mimetic* nature' (Lacoue-Labarthe 1978: 12). Here, then, according to Lacoue-Labarthe, is the cornerstone of

Girard's theory, which Lacoue-Labarthe encapsulates and, in a significant way, interprets through what I see as the influence of Lacan:

> every desire is desire of the other (and not immediately desire
> of an object), every structure of desire is triangular (including
> the other – mediator or model – whose desire desire imitates),
> every desire is thus from its inception tapped by hatred and
> rivalry; in short, the origin of desire is mimesis – mimeticism
> – and no desire is ever forged which does not desire forthwith
> the death or the disappearance of the model or 'exemplary'
> character which gave rise to it. This is why, for Girard
> [1972: 967], 'mimesis meets violence and violence redoubles
> mimesis'. Desire wants difference and autonomy, properness
> [*le propre*] and property, it is the very will to decision; the
> Same (identity, identification, indifferentiation) is its terror
> and the evil which gnaws away at it. Because desire's obsession
> is originality, desire wants its origin negated and its essence
> forgotten. . . . What is essential . . . lies in this belonging-
> together, of the kind we have just observed, of mimesis, desire,
> and rivalry. What is essential is the violent power of mimesis,
> not only inasmuch as desire is mimesis but, much more fun-
> damentally perhaps, inasmuch as mimesis provokes desire. For
> it is finally an intuition of this sort which animates Plato's
> 'psychology'.
>
> (Lacoue-Labarthe 1978: 12)

Lacoue-Labarthe's rephrasing of Girard points to what for me is the major difficulty of Girard's work: his use of key terms such as mimesis, desire, rivalry and violence. Girard is persistent, and I think very intentionally so, in his refusal to be restrictive in his use of these terms or to define the precise relationship of the terms. They are, he tells us repeatedly, 'closely related'. In Lacoue-Labarthe's words, what is important is 'this belonging-together', yet Lacoue-Labarthe reveals the natural impulse to say more about 'this belonging-together' than Girard will allow. By specifying what is 'closely related' in terms of direct equations and causal relation, Lacoue-Labarthe has perhaps 'decided' for Girard, despite Girard's adherence to the 'indecidability' of his terms. The equations and causal relations constructed by Lacoue-Labarthe create their own set of problems: 'desire is mimesis', and 'mimesis provokes desire'.

Lacoue-Labarthe suggests that Girard fails to recognize sufficiently his indebtedness to Plato by ascribing to the 'great writers' (Cervantes, Dostoevsky, Shakespeare, etc.) a 'quasi-theory of mimetic desire, absent in Plato and in antiquity, and once again suppressed in the modern period' (quoted and translated by Lacoue-Labarthe 1978: 13 from Girard 1972: 963). In Girard's defence I would note that Girard certainly acknowledges that for Plato mimesis, particularly in the form of tragedy, inspired great fear. What Plato failed to understand, according to Girard, (and what would be, I think, Girard's response to Lacoue-Labarthe) is that disorder and violence in tragedy are closely related to – can in fact even become synonymous with – peace and harmony, through the mechanism of unanimous victimage.

In *Violence and the Sacred*, Girard (1977a: 4) describes the scapegoat as 'a relatively indifferent victim' who is sufficiently marginalized in the social community so that 'his' sacrifice does not elicit filial retaliation. In other words, the degree of integration within the social community first determines whether an individual can function as the scapegoat (Girard 1977a: 4–13). Although women are marginalized members of the community, they do not often serve as scapegoats because they are the property of men and their sacrifice would thus elicit retaliation, perpetuating the violence which the sacrifice must resolve. Nevertheless, as sexuality is closely linked to violence and as violence, like the female in menses and in childbirth, is associated with bloodshed, women, through a process of symbolization may well receive the blame for all violence. In fact, Girard (1977a: 36) detects 'some half-suppressed desire to place the blame for all forms of violence on women'. As procreation is associated with, necessitated by, death, the female body or the woman *per se* becomes the Janus figure of life and death, womb and tomb.

Contesting Girard's notion of the 'relatively indifferent' identity of the scapegoat, Lacoue-Labarthe affirms the validity of Plato's insistence upon the poet as the primary agent of mimesis and thus the perfect *pharmakos*. The scapegoat qualifies for 'his' role to the extent that he is the representative or bearer of mimesis:

> For it is quite necessary, in the rejection of the 'bearer of mimesis,' that the victim incarnate in one way or another this im-propriety [*im-propriété*], this lack of being-proper necessarily supposed, as Plato knows very well, by the mimetic fact – that is, not only the indifferentiation and endless doubling that threaten the social organism as a whole, but, on an underlying level and actually provoking them, mimeticism itself, this pure and disquieting *plasticity* which authorized potentially the changing appropriation of all the characters and all the functions (all the roles), this kind of 'typical virtuosity' which doubtless

requires a 'subjective' underpinning – a 'wax' – but without any other property than an infinite malleability: *instability* 'itself.' It is then entirely necessary for the scapegoat to incarnate what Girard aims to convey *under* the name of the 'undifferentiated,' which is the general absence of identity.... The victim is always, whatever 'his' status, a *mimos* . . . who exhibits 'his' non-identity, who brings along in 'his' story (Oedipus) or 'his' function (the king), in 'his' *ethos* (the fool) or 'his' trade (the actor, the artist), the dreaded evidence of the primal status and undivided rule of mimetic confusion.

(Lacoue-Labarthe 1978: 20–21)

Lacoue-Labarthe concludes that the scapegoat is thus 'a specialist' of mimesis, one who in showing 'himself' shows himself to be 'at once everything – and nothing' (Lacoue-Labarthe 1978: 21). 'He' is a monster in the double sense of a show, demonstration, or representation of that which is monstrous: the 'undifferentiated'. In the discussion of *Antony and Cleopatra* that follows, I will show the extent to which Cleopatra qualifies for the role of scapegoat as Lacoue-Labarthe here describes it.

For Lacoue-Labarthe (1978: 21), the 'oldest and most constant gesture *vis-à-vis* mimesis' is the attempt 'to reveal it by staging it. . . . Far from covering up or masking mimesis, theatricality "reveals" it'. The tendency of the theatre in Shakespeare's day to dis-cover or represent the mechanism of mimesis in terms of desire, rivalry and violence surely accounts for much of the hostility towards the theatre now commonly referred to as the antitheatrical bias found most prevalently in the Puritan polemics of the period. The theatre's revelation of mimesis perhaps in large part explains why for Girard 'the play's the thing', rather than some other genre. The subject of theatrical mimesis is the mimetic mechanism within human nature, or, in Girard's terms, the mimetic endeavour of the theatre is 'mimetic revelation'. The intertextual and highly self-reflexive or 'metadramatical' nature of Shakespeare's plays designates them as both theory and practice of mimetic revelation.

The value of Girard's theory of mimesis is apparent not only in his own application of it to literary texts, particularly to the plays of Shakespeare, but also in its influence upon other literary critics. The finest example of this influence is in the long, complex essay by Joel Fineman, 'Fratricide and Cuckoldry: Shakespeare's Doubles' (1977). Part of Fineman's objective is to explain the relationship of androgyny and cuckoldry to fratricidal rivalry, and the relevance of this relationship to Shakespeare's plays. Like the reciprocal violence that defines antagonists as doubles or brothers, androgyny and cuckoldry belie the myth of difference inscribed in gender roles and in exclusive possession. Fineman (1977: 422) sees most clearly in *Hamlet* 'a connection between alternately shifting sex roles, male and female disguise, madness and androgyny' which depends 'upon a consistent language of misogyny whose grammar inexorably links female unfaithfulness to fratricidal violence'. In a brilliant extension of Girard's theory, Fineman (1977: 432) argues that

> [t]he dialectic of Difference and No Difference contained in the original fratricide structure is transferred by Shakespeare to another formula of mirroring reciprocity, to themes of women and their 'frailty,' to a kind of masculine misogyny that finds in the ambiguity of woman its own self-divided self-consciousness, its own vulnerability, its mortality.

This statement calls to mind Girard's insight into the 'half-suppressed desire to place the blame for all forms of violence on women' – an insight that should be of particular interest to psychoanalytic and feminist critics alike.[2]

What is perhaps most outstanding about Girard's theory is its relevance or applicability not only to disparate literary approaches but also to many disparate traditional disciplines: history, philosophy, sociology, anthropology and psychology. In the interview with *Diacritics* (Girard 1978a), later incorporated in *'To Double Business Bound'* (Girard 1978b: 199–229), Girard notes the numerous attempts to appropriate his theory, or at least, the 'temptation' to do so. He mentions specifically Lacoue-Labarthe's 'Typographe' in *Mimésis des articulations* (1975), excerpts of which were also published in *Diacritics* and discussed above. As a professor of philosophy and author of a study on Lacanian psychoanalysis, Lacoue-Labarthe attests to the interest Girard's theory generates in scholars of disparate disciplines. The interface between Girard's theory and psychoanalysis is, I believe, particularly important, as his commentaries on Freud illustrate. Girard's argument (1977a: 170–71) that the male child's rivalry with the father is in place prior to any sexual cathexis toward the mother, that the boy's identification with the father is 'anterior to any object choice', constitutes a serious challenge to the theory of the Oedipus complex. The mechanism of mimesis invites a thorough revision of our understanding of human motivation as it deconstructs the myth of the autonomous subject.

Girard's hypotheses, like those of Freudian and post-Freudian psychoanalysis, deal with the complex interconnectedness of death and desire, but without submerging the reader in the highly technical jargon and elaborate schemes characteristic of psychoanalytic theory. Despite the play of key terms, Girard's style is extremely confident and clear – free of what he identifies in the style of many post-structuralists as the *'valse hésitation'* (Girard 1978a: 51) – what I take to mean a style dominated by ambivalence and qualification that mystifies more than it clarifies. Girard has, in fact, been criticized for his confidence in his ability to find the 'truth of the text' – that is, for his assumption that the 'author' understands his own intentions and that as reader Girard, in turn, understands the author. The 'truth of the text' that Girard persistently seeks and finds is the author's understanding of the operations of mimesis. Paisley Livingston ('Girard and Literary Knowledge', in Juilland 1986: 222–3) notes that in the tide of post-structuralist doubt, Girard appears to cling to the rock of referentiality, with his emphasis upon the cognitive value of literature. In Girard's defence, Livingston states:

> At a time when it is increasingly taken for granted that real knowledge is not typically produced within the faculty of the arts and humanities at all, but is the product of the sciences, an argument for the cognitive importance of literature takes on much wider implications. . . . Girard's approach is promising, then, insofar as it could free literary studies from the intellectual ghetto where they are today firmly positioned, or more precisely, allowed to subsist for all the wrong reasons. That Girard's ideas, having been developed initially through literary analyses, are now being taken up by various researchers in a number of disciplines, suggests that he is one of a few contemporary thinkers whose work has seriously challenged the established opposition between the 'two cultures'.
>
> (Juilland 1986: 227–8)

II

Antony and Cleopatra is in a profound sense the sequel to *Julius Caesar*, for the 'foundational violence' of Caesar's murder is but temporarily resolved with the union in death of Caesar and Brutus at the end of *Julius Caesar*. The ritualized sacrifice of Caesar not only fails to secure the Republic but also generates the triumvirate and the civil war, which culminates in the battle at Philippi with the death of Brutus. With the eulogies of Antony and Octavius, Brutus is transformed from conspirator to 'noblest Roman of them all', united with his 'lover' Caesar in the sacrifice that brings together opposing forces in their reverence for 'the same double-headed god' (Girard 1991: 201). The resulting peace is, however, clearly ephemeral; no longer united against a common adversary, Antony and Octavius will inevitably become hostile rivals. Their rivalry is, in fact, in place before Brutus has found his resting-place. The violence begun on the ides of March will end only with the death of Antony and the ascendence of Octavius as *the* Roman Emperor. Antony and Cleopatra come together within the context of the rivalry between two Roman brothers who divide the world between them. The coming together and the togetherness of Antony and Cleopatra can, in fact, be understood only within the complex patterns of mimetic desire and rivalry that govern action and characterization in *Antony and Cleopatra*.

Cleopatra's first words, 'If it be love indeed, tell me how much' (I.i.14), suggest that desire is mimetic: measured against and generated by a model. Antony's love is also already contextualized within the polarity of Egypt and Rome and specifically within a rivalry between Cleopatra and her doubled adversary, 'scarce-bearded' Caesar and Fulvia. The play opens with a conflict, a lover's quarrel and Cleopatra's 'wrangling'. Her taunts are designed to elicit from Antony a display of difference; she attempts to provoke the 'masculine protest'.[3] Specifically, she defines Antony's masculinity as under erasure through his submission to a boy and a woman, Octavius and Fulvia, both of whom appropriate the role of a man. The similarity between these rivals, Egypt and Rome, resides in their shared assumption that the other is a threat to Antony's masculinity. The Roman perspective is articulated by Philo in his choric prologue and reiterated by Octavius: Antony 'is not more manlike/Than Cleopatra, nor the queen of Ptolemy/More womanly than he' (I.iv.5–7). Antony affirms the Roman perspective as well:

> I must from this enchanting queen break off:
> Ten thousand harms, more than the ills I know,
> My idleness doth hatch . . .
>
> (I.ii.128–30)

Cleopatra's charm, like Oberon's, is 'love-in-idleness' (*A Midsummer Night's Dream*, II.i.168), but Antony equates his idleness with the serpent and consoles himself with the thought that the harms hatched by his idleness do not yet have 'a serpent's poison' (I.ii.193). Cleopatra is Antony's 'serpent of old Nile' (I.v.25) and 'Idleness itself' (I.iii.94). For Antony's soldiers, Actium becomes 'Ten thousand harms' and the consequence of becoming 'women's men' (III.vii.70). Within the

binary opposition constructed under the signifiers Rome and Egypt,
Shakespeare dramatizes the anxiety of differentiation that defines
gender and ethnicity.

Antony is the split, duplicitous subject caught not only between the
polarities of Egypt and Rome but also, more significantly, between
the imperatives of two different types of rivalry: what Girard calls
internal and external. He attempts to respond to Cleopatra's opening
enquiry and demand by recontextualizing his love in terms of an
external rivalry:

> Let Rome in Tiber melt, and the wide arch
> Of the ranged empire fall! Here is my space.
> Kingdoms are clay. Our dungy earth alike
> Feeds beast as man. The nobleness of life
> Is to do thus, [*embracing Cleopatra*] when such a mutual pair
> And such a twain can do't – in which I bind,
> On pain of punishment. the world to weet
> We stand up peerless.
>
> (I.i.35–42)

He thus claims to renounce the objects of internal rivalry – Rome,
empire, kingdoms, all that is 'dungy earth' – for the achievement
within an external rivalry through which he and Cleopatra 'stand up
peerless' in their difference. Their desire is mimetic, mediated by the
desire of gods, 'the love of Love' (I.i.46). Their models are none other
than the gods and legendary lovers: Venus and Mars, Isis and Osiris,
Dido and Aeneas.[4] Cleopatra defines even more clearly than Antony
the external model for their mimetic desire:

> Eternity was in our lips and eyes,
> Bliss in our brows bent; none our parts so poor,
> But was a race of heaven.
>
> (I.iii.35–7)

Within this external rivalry, there is no risk of generating violence,
for the models and rivals inhabit a remote space, a different world.

Unlike Antony, Cleopatra is quick to acknowledge that her desire
is also an integral part of an internal rivalry with Fulvia and Octavius.
As the rival who displaces Fulvia, Cleopatra acknowledges Fulvia as
her double. Antony is 'Excellent falsehood' (I.i.42), for his former
betrayal of Fulvia prefigures for Cleopatra Antony's imminent betrayal
of her (I.i.40–42). Observing Antony's indifferent response to the
news of Fulvia's death, Cleopatra again identifies her former rival as

her double: 'Now I see, I see,/In Fulvia's death how mine received shall be' (I.iii.64–5). Antony's marriage to Octavia confirms his 'Excellent falsehood', as well as Cleopatra's realization that desire and rivalry are doubles in their reciprocal generation. Whereas one might expect Antony's betrayal of Cleopatra through his marriage to Octavia to nullify or at least qualify her desire for him, the effect is quite the opposite. The marriage merely intensifies Cleopatra's desire as it provides her with a new, living rival. 'All may be well enough' (III.iii.46) for Cleopatra precisely because through this new rivalry Cleopatra defines difference: her superior beauty, wit and sexual attraction. Like Enobarbus, Cleopatra knows Antony 'will to his Egyptian dish again' (II.vi.125).

Antony's declaration of the difference achieved by 'such a mutual pair' belies the risk implicit in this mutuality: the androgynous fusion and confusion of identities. Such confusion is suggested when Enobarbus says, 'Hush, here comes Anthony,' and Charmian responds, 'Not he, the Queen' (I.ii.78) and also when Cleopatra and Antony, in their cross-dressing, replay the myth of Hercules and Omphale (II.v.21–3). In fact, Antony shares the Roman fear that, coupled with Cleopatra, he has lost distinction or difference: all that sets him apart from and above other men within a well-established matrix of internal rivalry. He is a part of the Roman world where three at the top, the triumvirate, have failed to establish Degree. The rivalries and the reciprocal violence laid to rest at the end of *Julius Caesar* are reborn and constitute the context within which Antony must define difference, despite his declarations made to Cleopatra to the contrary. Labienus, who supported Brutus and Cassius against the triumvirate, threatens once more; Fulvia, allied with her erstwhile enemy, Antony's brother Lucius, has raised an army against Octavius; 'Equality of two domestic powers/Breed scrupulous faction' (I.iii.47–8) as Sextus Pompeius seeks retribution for his father. Thus with Antony's return to Rome the internal rivalries of the immediate and temporal take precedence over the idealized external rivalries through which the mimetic desire of the peerless 'mutual pair' is constituted.

With Antony's return to Rome and his efforts to reconcile his differences with Octavius, the young Caesar appears victorious in his rivalry with Cleopatra for the possession of Antony. Octavius finds in his sister, whose name is so like his own, the perfect surrogate through which he may claim Antony, the desired object. But Antony is also for Octavius the rival and model for emulation, the soldier's soldier, as Octavius's tribute (I.iv.55–71) makes clear. The match between Antony and Octavia is thus designed to establish Degree either by making the two rivals, Antony and Octavius, 'as one' in marriage or by providing the cause for one rival to triumph over the other and thus to assert difference and ascendence through violent conflict.

The temporary union of Octavius and Antony, sealed by the marriage between Octavia and Antony, serves merely to clear the ground, eliminating Sextus Pompeius and Lepidus, for the arch rivalry between Octavius and Antony. Heeding the advice of the Soothsayer, Antony attempts to forestall this rivalry by returning to Egypt and thus placing distance between himself and Octavius. Enobarbus, however, provides the choric commentary on this rivalry that has been escalating since the defeat of Brutus:

> Then, world, thou hast a pair of chops, no more,
> And throw between them all the food thou hast,
> They'll grind the one the other.
>
> (III.v.12–14)

Upon Antony's return to Egypt, he and Cleopatra play out the external rivalry, their emulation of the divine model; 'on a tribunal silvered' and 'in chairs of gold' (III.vi.3–4), she 'In th'habiliments of the goddess Isis' (III.vi.17), they define their peerless status. But kingdoms are not clay; they are the signifiers of difference within internal rivalries as, according to Octavius, Antony makes Cleopatra absolute Queen of Egypt, lower Syria, Cyprus and Lydia. This gift of kingdoms – 'He hath given his empire/Up to a whore' (III.vi.66–7) – is for Octavius sufficient cause for war. Caught between the external rivalry with a divine model and the internal rivalry with Octavius, Antony attempts to affirm the ideal inherent in the former as he confronts the violence of the latter. Cleopatra is his 'Thetis' for whom he at the battle of Actium puts aside the pragmatics of warfare to meet Caesar's forces at sea. But the dynamics of internal rivalry with Caesar govern Antony as well; asked to explain the decision to fight at sea, Antony answers, 'For that he dares us to't' (III.vii.29).

At the battle of Actium, Enobarbus sees the risk inherent in androgynous union and thus insists upon separation of the sexes and the distinction of gender roles; feminine sexuality can only deter the will to achieve within male rivalry. Cleopatra, however, asserts an ideal androgyny; as president of her nation she will 'Appear there for a man' (III.vii.18). When under fire she fails to do so, Cleopatra and Antony ironically redefine their mutuality by their cowardly flight from the battle. With the defeat, Antony loses his distinction among men, upon which his sense of difference and worth is predicated. The ideal of androgynous union, of the 'Mutual pair', gives way to the return of his repressed Roman fear of a feminine sexuality that emasculates. To Cleopatra's sexuality Antony accords 'full supremacy' (III.xi.58) and thus accounts for his sword 'made weak by [his] affection' (III.xi.66). In Enobarbus's more cynical language, 'The itch of his affection' has 'nicked his captainship' (III.xiii.7–8). 'Salt Cleopatra' (II.i.21) has made yet another Roman warrior lay his sword to bed. Antony can retrieve his manhood only by differentiating himself from Cleopatra through the blame he transfers to her. Although Enobarbus assures Cleopatra that 'Anthony only' (III.xiii.3) is at fault, Cleopatra, through her appeal for pardon and her womanly tears, facilitates Antony's effort to distinguish himself from her. With his magnanimous forgiveness – 'Fall not a tear, I say: one of them rates/All that is won and lost' (III.xi.68–9) – Antony reaffirms the worth of Cleopatra and thus the transcendence of their desire. But he does so now with a difference, for he distinguishes himself from Cleopatra through the power and the perfidity he ascribes to her sexuality.

The famous tribute to Cleopatra offered by Enobarbus provides the clue to what is so frightening for Antony about Cleopatra's sexuality:

Age cannot wither her, nor custom stale
Her infinite variety; other women cloy
The appetites they feed, but she makes hungry
Where most she satisfies; for vilest things
Become themselves in her, that the holy priests
Bless her when she is riggish.

(II.ii.242–7)

On a superficial level, this speech says that Cleopatra's sexual appeal transcends time and use – that the more she is used the more she elicits desire. Vilest things are so becoming in her that even her wantonness is sacred. Upon closer inspection, the syntactically peculiar word here is the coordinating conjunction, 'for', in that it suggests a causal relation between her power to generate an insatiable appetite in others and the vilest things in herself. This construction invites the possibility that vilest things are not simply becoming in her but become what they are, 'Become themselves', through her. Furthermore, as Antony's subjectivity is constituted through his desire for Cleopatra, his desire is also associated with 'vilest things'; through mimetic confusion, he becomes himself and one with 'vilest things'. Within the context of the words 'vilest things' and 'riggish', the words 'custom' and 'stale' evoke supplementary meanings relevant to the play as a whole. The word 'stale' in this passage is a verb, meaning to make stale, and has the contextual association familiar to a modern reader with food, feeding and appetite. The word in this context thus offers an ironic gloss upon Cleopatra's 'If it be love indeed' (I.i.14). As a verb and a noun, 'stale' also refers to urine, particularly in reference to horses, as Octavius's line, 'Thou didst drink/The stale of horses' (I.iv.61–2) illustrates. At Actium Enobarbus would have no mare among the horses (III.vii.7–10), and Cleopatra becomes the 'ribanded nag of Egypt' (III.x.10). 'Stale' is also a common term for prostitute, and for one who is exploited and rejected within a rivalry – what Antony imagines himself to be when Cleopatra becomes the stale. In addition to its modern meaning, the word 'custom' had in the Renaissance a meaning, now obsolete, in reference to women. As the Geneva and King James versions of the Bible illustrate, 'the custom of woman' refers to menstruation (Genesis 31: 35), a condition that, according to some traditions, makes her vile or unclean, and, according to Girard, associates her through bloodshed with all forms of violence. The terms of Enobarbus's glorious tribute thus contain the trace of Antony's deepest anxieties and repressed Roman thoughts about Cleopatra's sexuality. Never in her impropriety the exclusive property of any man, she generates rivalry among men, just as she generates desire. Her excess, her uncontained sexuality, is both blessing and curse, medicine and poison. His later assessment of her as the 'Triple-turned whore' (IV.xiii.13) suggests that for Antony custom or use has indeed staled her, that she is 'a morsel, cold upon/Dead Caesar's trencher' (III.xiii.117–18).

Monstrous androgyny, feminine sexuality, and woman's frailty thus become the conflated same and the threat to masculinity and to the achievement of distinction or difference among men. As sexual difference depends upon the myth of feminine frailty, the woman must betray the man if he is to preserve his distinction from her. For this reason, misogyny is essential to the male's fashioning of his sexual identity. Yet in her betrayal as she renders him the cuckold, she defines all men as the same. As Benedick in *Much Ado About Nothing* suggests, women create the brotherhood of men, first in men's resistance to marriage and finally in married men's acceptance that 'There is no staff more reverend than one tipped with horn' (V.iv.123–4). Such comic accommodation to the threat of cuckoldry does not exist in the tragedies. Instead, woman's frailty necessitates or is responsible for fratricidal rivalry; as a woman's frailty undermines a man's distinction among men, he must perpetually reassert or attempt to achieve that distinction through rivalry. Once Antony distinguishes himself from Cleopatra through her frailty and the magnanimity it enables, his conviction of her subsequent betrayal is inevitable.

Cleopatra, once the rival of Octavius for the possession of Antony, becomes, like the world itself, the object of a rivalry between as Theobald had it in 1733, 'a pair of chaps'. After the battle at Actium and Antony's humble acknowledgement of defeat (III.xii.12–15), Octavius resolves to 'win Cleopatra' from Antony (III.xii.28). Since this scarce-bearded youth is the only Roman consistently immune to the charms of Cleopatra, his true desire appears to be revenge against one who rejected him and against one for whom he was rejected. His misogynistic assessment of this 'whore' through whom his revenge will work anticipates success: 'Women are not/In their best fortunes strong; but want will perjure/The ne'er-touched vestal' (III.xii. 30–2). Antony's violent and vituperative response to the efforts of Thidias, Caesar's messenger, to win Cleopatra (III.xiii.85–153) reveals that Antony and Octavius are doubles not only in their fratricidal rivalry but also in their misogyny. The shifts with such celerity from trust to distrust, from love to hate and back again to love, suggest that for Antony love and hate are also doubles. Antony's rage is once again against the threat of 'no difference'. Thidias's familiarity with Cleopatra's hand is a violation of Degree and thus of that peerless status that distinguishes Cleopatra and Antony. Her complicity in this violation obliterates her name – 'what's her name,/Since she was Cleopatra?' (III.xiii.98–9) – as it moves Antony to declare, 'I am/ Anthony yet' (III.xiii.92–3).

Cleopatra's conciliatory question, 'Not know me yet?' (III.xiii.158), ironically emphasizes the fact that Antony knows her only within the Roman polarities: as the goddess of Enobarbus's tributes and as the whore of Octavius's and his own insults. She is the Other he can know only within the constructs of his own imaginary projections, where she functions both as ego ideal and as scapegoat. In Lacan's terms, the subject 'can never reach its sexual partner, which is the Other, except by way of mediation, as the cause of its desire'. ('A love letter', in Mitchell and Rose 1982: 151). Antony's knowledge of Cleopatra as 'a boggler' (III.xiii.111), as 'a morsel, cold upon/Dead Caesar's trencher', as 'a fragment/Of Gneius Pompey's' (III.xiii.117–19), as one who can but 'guess what temperance should be' (III.xiii.122), and as the 'Triple-turned whore' (IV.xiii.13) clearly inscribes her within the context of fratricidal rivalry. Fineman's (1977: 432) observation of the connection between fratricide and 'frailty' in *Hamlet* applies perfectly to *Antony and Cleopatra*:

The dialectic of Difference and No Difference contained in the original fratricide structure is transferred by Shakespeare to another formula of mirroring reciprocity, to themes of women and their 'frailty,' to a kind of masculine misogyny that finds in the ambiguity of woman its own self-divided self-consciousness, its own vulnerability, its mortality.

And certainly in his misogynistic conviction of Cleopatra's betrayal, Antony meets as in a mirror his own multitudinous betrayals.

The lie of Cleopatra's suicide forces Antony to see Cleopatra's betrayal as his own projection. Absolving her of frailty, he will assume the woman's part she played after their flight at Actium: 'I will o'ertake thee, Cleopatra, and/Weep for my pardon' (IV.xv.44–5). He again conceives of a mutual pair, peerless in their mimetic rivalry with the gods and with the lovers of legend:

Where souls do couch on flowers we'll hand in hand,
And with our sprightly port make the ghosts gaze.
Dido and her Aeneas shall want troops,
And all the haunt be ours. Come, Eros, Eros!

(IV.xv.51–4)

Before falling upon his sword, Antony speaks the name of Eros 15 times within 102 lines – a repetition that surely invokes the god of desire whose name his soldier shares. With his suicide, Eros, like Cleopatra, becomes the model for Antony's emulation and thus his rival within a pattern of external rivalry: 'Eros,/Thy master dies thy scholar' (IV.xv.101–2). Whereas in Act I, Antony's duplicity is figured as a conflict between external and internal rivalries, now, as he mimes his external models, Cleopatra and Eros, he defeats his internal rival, Octavius.

Caesar's response to the news of Antony's death makes clear that the fratricidal violence of internal rivalry evolves not out of Difference but out of No Difference – out of the anxiety over sameness or the absence of distinction. 'Caesar is touched': he sheds tears now for Antony as he did for Brutus. Mecenas explains, 'When such a spacious mirror's set before him,/He needs must see himself' (V.i.34–5). In his encomium for Antony, Caesar not only sees himself but acknowledges the true objective of the conflict between doubles:

O Anthony,
I have followed thee to this; but we do lance
Diseases in our bodies. I must perforce
Have shown to thee such a declining day,
Or look on thine: we could not stall together
In the whole world. But yet let me lament

With tears as sovereign as the blood of hearts
That thou, my brother, my competitor
In top of all design, my mate in empire,
Friend and companion in the front of war,
The arm of mine own body, and the heart
Where mine his thoughts did kindle – that our stars
Unreconcilable should divide
Our equalness to this.

                                        (V.i.35–48)

Here is the perfect text for Girard's theory of mimetic desire and rivalry
and of the violence that seeks to establish difference. Caesar here
acknowledges the admiration, the esteem, he has all along felt for
Antony that allows Antony to become his model, the mediator of his
desire, and thus his rival. From Antony's heart is kindled the desire
of Caesar, and precisely because they – like Proteus and Valentine,
Caesar and Brutus – are friends and and brothers, they are rivals.
Clearly, it is not their 'stars' (fate or a supernatural influence) that
divide their 'equalness' but their own aversion to that 'equalness' that
belies difference within a crisis of Degree.

   Certain phrases of Caesar's encomium – 'my mate in empire', 'Friend
and companion', 'the heart/Where mine his thoughts did kindle' – also
suggest a homo-erotic attachment which complicates this rivalry.
Antony has been for Caesar both the rival double or brother, as well
as the object of desire in Caesar's rivalry with Cleopatra. Because
Caesar's triumph over Antony is qualified by Antony's suicide, his
conquest of Cleopatra must serve as both compensation and retaliation.
To lead in triumph the last great enemy of the empire and the woman
who captured the heart of his lover-rival would, in fact, more than
compensate; as Caesar says, 'her life in Rome/Would be eternal in
our triumph' (V.i.65–6).

   The victor is, however, vanquished within Cleopatra's dream of
an Emperor Antony. Through her imaginative revisioning, Antony
achieves apotheosis to join the 'race of heaven' (I.iii.37) whose desires
the lovers emulate. He thus becomes the model for her own emulation
within the pattern of external rivalry, precisely as she became the
model for him within the lie of her suicide. Through her emulation,
Cleopatra conceives her own liberation and elevation. No longer the
object to be possessed within the internal rivalry of Caesar and Antony,
she now displaces Caesar to become the immortal friend and 'competitor' (a word meaning 'partner' in the Renaissance) of Antony.
The courage that enables her suicide 'after the high Roman fashion'

(IV.xvi.88) of Antony not only earns her the right to claim Antony as her husband but also allows him to 'mock/The luck of Caesar' (V.ii.284–5). Thus through her emulation of Antony within an external rivalry she confirms Antony's defeat of Octavius within the frame of their internal rivalry.

Her resolution is transformative:

> I have nothing
> Of woman in me – now from head to foot
> I am marble constant; now the fleeting moon
> No planet is of mine.
> . . .
> I am fire and air – my other elements
> I give to baser life.
>
> (V.ii.238–41, 288–9)

What must be transcended in this effort to rival Antony is the frailty or inconstancy consistently ascribed in the play to woman. Like the anti-Semitism of *The Merchant of Venice*, the anti-feminism inscribed here as the frailty of woman appears to be both thematic and structural, both interrogated by and complicitously reflected in the play. The baser cold elements, earth and water, are associated, like the Nile and its ooze, with corporeal Cleopatra and with woman *per se*.

Despite the mimetic endeavour, Cleopatra's suicide is not at all 'after the high Roman fashion'. In fact, its decidedly Egyptian fashion reinscribes her feminine sexuality: the 'joy of the worm' (V.ii.259) and her 'celerity in dying' (I.ii.143) – that which attracts and repels, entices and terrifies, unmans the man in the very act of making *him*. With her 'baby' at her breast (V.ii.308–10), Cleopatra becomes once more Antony's 'serpent of old Nile' (I.v.25) whose poison is mortal and immortal. At this moment of her own transmigration, she is associated with another 'serpent' of the Nile, the crocodile, a monster of non-differentiation:

> It is shaped, sir, like itself, and it is as broad as it hath breadth.
> It is just so high as it is, and moves with it own organs. It lives
> by that which nourisheth it, and the elements once out of it,
> it transmigrates.
>
> (II.vii.41–4)

The image of Cleopatra with her 'baby' at the breast is surely a dramatic *tour de force* that Shakespeare could not resist. The image, however, is not altogether his own creation. Although none of Shakespeare's sources, as we know them, places the serpent at

Cleopatra's breast, there was clearly a literary and iconographic tradition that did.[5] Shakespeare's decision to place the asp at Cleopatra's breast and to underscore the image with her deictic lines, 'Dost thou not see my baby at my breast,/That sucks the nurse asleep?' (V.ii.308-9) is motivated, I believe, by more than a sense of the dramatic or the sensational. This, her last question and virtually her last lines, recalls her earlier question to Antony, 'Not know me yet?'. The 'baby' at her breast obviously defines Cleopatra's courage, resolve and wit, but it also establishes her within a familiar emblematic, allegorical tradition. Nursing the serpent suggests the engendering of it. Woman's procreative power, her sexuality, is thus connected to death and to the transgression that necessitates death. The serpent at the breast deconstructs madonna and child to reaffirm the intimacy between the serpent and Eve, an intimacy definitively expressed in paintings of the Middle Ages and Renaissance in which the serpent's face mirrors the face of Eve. Michaelangelo's depiction in the Sistine Chapel of the temptation of Eve is perhaps the most familiar example. This particular 'baby' at Cleopatra's breast evokes a tradition to which belong the offspring of Spenser's Error, of Milton's Sin, and of Lear's fearful imaginings of what is engendered below the waist of woman. Thus the misogynistic bias of the male characters in *Antony and Cleopatra*, reflected in their fear and distrust and in the projection of their own duplicity upon Cleopatra – a bias that Shakespeare has effectively interrogated throughout the play – seems suddenly to be affirmed with the final detail of her characterization.

But Cleopatra's final performance that transforms the asp into the baby at her breast is also her final jest, an act of play and of play-making, that, with its fusion of joy, tranquillity, tenderness and mockery, escapes both polarized images of the woman that it conjures. In other words, this performance deconstructs the negative, anti-feminist image of Eve and the serpent as surely as it does the beatific image of madonna and child. The jest thus locates the nature of Cleopatra outside both the negative and positive male construct of woman, fashioned by characters within the play and by critics who accept either construct.

If, within these constructs, she 'is not', what is she? Those who love her and those who hate her, within the play-world and within the critical debates, are united in their recognition of her as the consummate performer, as the embodiment of theatricality itself: all that is and is not. As Cleopatra is to the male characters 'a wonderful piece of work', she is to the playwright the symbol – figuring product and process – of his own mimetic endeavour. She is the *mimos*, the bearer of mimesis. Her infinite variety, a polymorphous sexuality that perpetually elicits the mimetic desire of the other, is uncontained and uncontainable; its instability – her riggishness – is the mark of the sacred. In her infinite variety she, thus, in a double sense, embodies im-propriety, the lack of being proper and of being one man's exclusive property. In her plasticity, her infinite malleability, she represents the threat of no difference or of instability, itself. As the bearer of mimesis and the embodiment of monstrous non-differentiation, Cleopatra is the *pharmakon*. Like the serpent's sting, she is both poison and remedy.

Through her ritualized sacrifice she becomes, in the words of the clown, 'a dish for the gods' (V.ii.273). Her death thus ends the mimetic violence that began with the earlier effort at ritual sacrifice signified in the resolve to carve Julius Caesar 'as a dish fit for the gods' (*Julius Caesar*, II.i.173). The internal rivalry settled, Cleopatra is at last allowed her own distinction as 'A lass unparalleled' (V.ii.314) who 'would catch another Anthony/In her strong toil of grace' (V.ii.345–6). Caesar can finally afford to the lovers the distinction they sought through their external rivalry: 'No grave upon the earth shall clip in it/A pair so famous' (V.ii.357–8).

Although, as I hope I have shown, *Antony and Cleopatra* perfectly illustrates René Girard's theory of mimetic desire and rivalry to the extent that it may justly be called a quasi-theoretical text, the play deviates substantially from Girard's theory of unanimous or collective victimage. Although the suicides of the lovers appear as ritualized sacrifice that puts an end to violence, Antony and Cleopatra are not the victims of an act of murder. Their sacrifice of life is an offering of each to the other that radically deviates from the pattern of sacrificial violence Girard finds in many great tragedies. At the same time, it would be very difficult to find a literary character who better fits Girard's and Lacoue-Labarthe's delineation of the *pharmakon* than Cleopatra. As her 'infinite variety' defies definition and containment, she is the embodiment of mimeticism.

The triumph and transcendence, levity and joy, and the absence of any sense of guilt or expiation with which Cleopatra stages her suicide surely account in large part for the singularity of this late tragedy and for the fact that literary critics have tended to exclude it from the rank or list of Shakespeare's greatest tragedies. In fact, the play in various ways seems to frustrate generic expectations: to defy unity of action, dignity of character, and cathartic effect. The persistent irony generated by the disparity between the self-aggrandizing myths the protagonists generate and the deeds and motives that define them on-stage renders this play for many readers more parodic than tragic. For some critics (generally male), the binary opposition between Roman honour and duty and Egyptian self-indulgence and eroticism results in a reductive reading of Antony as one confronted with a choice between virtue and vice, who lacks the will to make the moral choice and thus pays the price for his 'dotage'. This 'Roman' perspective necessitates a blindness to various ways in which the play undermines its own binary construction as it reveals, for example, the treachery, hypocrisy and betrayal within the Roman world. The truly 'gaudy night' (III.xiii.183) is set not on Cleopatra's barge but aboard Antony's Roman ship.

Collapsing its own polarities to which Roman thought self-righteously clings, the play confronts the undifferentiated, and, like Cleopatra, resists hierarchies and containment. We as readers, on the other hand (like Polonius with his 'tragedy, comedy, history, pastoral, pastoral-comical, historical-pastoral, tragical-historical, tragical-comical-historical-pastoral' (*Hamlet*, II.ii.391–4), have perhaps become victims of our own taxonomies through which we construct our own comfortable hierarchical order, our own system of literary Degree. A curative for this particular reader malaise, René Girard is the perfect *pharmakon*, as he illuminates the mechanism of mimesis common to all genres and to all great literary works. Girard reveals the prevailing pattern – with no generic difference – of the anxiety of no difference. Antagonists of comedies and tragedies alike contend with each other because they are similar and desire to affirm difference, and because in their similarity they desire 'according to the other' (Girard 1965: 4–5).

SUPPLEMENT

NIGEL WOOD: Cleopatra's death seems by your account to be an apotheosis of her own selfhood (or at least of her perceived Egyptian qualities). What about Antony's 'failure'? Is he meant to highlight Roman shortcomings or merely his own?

BARBARA J. BAINES: Certainly I have suggested that Cleopatra's death constitutes an apotheosis of her selfhood, but I would emphasize the androgynous nature of this selfhood: in her mimesis of 'the high Roman fashion' (IV.xvi.88) that defines her as 'marble constant', having 'nothing/Of woman' (V.ii.238–40), she also becomes the 'lass unparalleled' (V.ii.314). In her death the polarity and conflict between Rome (the masculine) and Egypt (the feminine) are dissolved. Antony does indeed highlight Roman shortcomings in many ways. But Enobarbus, who functions as chorus to stress Antony's duplicities and failures, also finally defines Antony as the 'mine of bounty' (IV.vi.31) and thus as the embodiment of munificence. Antony's suicide differs from Cleopatra's in the sense that it is an expiation for his distrust of Cleopatra and for his flight at Actium that allows Caesar's victory. Clearly, Antony's efforts at apotheosis through suicide fall short of Cleopatra's. His suicide is, first of all, rather comically bungled, and he is obliged to urge Cleopatra,

> please your thoughts
> In feeding them with those my former fortunes,
> Wherein I lived the greatest prince o'th'world . . .
>
> (IV.xvi.54–6)

To the extent that Antony achieves apotheosis, he does so through Cleopatra's revisioning of him in her dream of 'an Emperor Anthony'. (V.ii.76)

NW: Girard's model for interpretation here seems to emerge from his perception of an author's *internal* mimetic strife. Shakespeare must describe this as a projection of 'his' own divided self, as, of course, his Antony and Cleopatra do not exist. Do you accept this?

BJB: Unlike Freud and many biographical critics, Girard is not interested in psychoanalysing Shakespeare. But certainly virtually all of Shakespeare's works attest to the psychic structure of the double and probably in some sense mirror the playwright's own divided self. In his earliest comedy, doubling is literalized and doubled by two sets of twins (Plautus gives us only one set). The psychic import of the pattern of doubling is expressed in terms that strike me as self-referential:

> I to the world am like a drop of water
> That in the ocean seeks another drop,
> Who, falling there to find his fellow forth,
> Unseen, inquisitive, confounds himself.
>
> (*The Comedy of Errors*, I.ii.35–8)

The sonnets are generally presumed to offer us the best insight into the psyche of the poet. We will never know whether the rival poet of the sonnets is a fictitious construct or a biographical reality. What we can be sure of is that he, like the dark lady, belongs to the pattern of mediated desire.

NW: How would you answer the questioner who tries to point out that the power of mimesis lies in its capacity to figure a reality available to all readers, that is, one that has not been constructed culturally?

BJB: First of all, I would agree with Lacan that the Real is precisely that which is beyond our systems of signification or symbolization and thus what we know as reality is always a cultural construct. Our entry into language and all other forms of representation is our entry into a cultural construct. But I would also agree with Girard's suggestion that mimesis is as basic (and thus transcultural) to human nature as the 'drives' defined by Freud. To the extent, then, that mimesis (art) figures or represents the mimetic mechanism in human nature, it has the power to represent what is recognizable to all readers within the same cultural construct or symbolic order as that of the artist.

NW: What role does consciousness or awareness play within Girard's scheme of mimesis?

BJB: Desiring subjects always function under the delusion that their desire is their own; the mimetic nature of their desire eludes them entirely. Although the disciple or imitator recognizes his desire as being in conflict with the desire of his model, he does not realize that his desire is generated 'according to the other'. The more similar the rival is, the more the likelihood of conflict and the more imperative the need to deny similarity. Only when the rival is finally vanquished can the imitator confront or acknowledge kinship. Girard explains in *Violence and the Sacred* (1977: 7) that the scapegoat mechanism depends essentially upon the celebrants' misrecognition.

NW: In what way and to what extent do you find Girard's theory useful or relevant to the current discourses within the academy?

BJB: Girard is the model for the interdisciplinary approach that the academy has come recently and somewhat belatedly to value. His theory is relevant to all forms of discourse on self and other and particularly to the current historicized studies of the ways in which woman as 'other' has been represented. Any scholar concerned with 'the matter of difference' – whether that difference pertains to gender, ethnicity, class, or something else – could gain valuable insights from René Girard.

CHAPTER 2

Representing Cleopatra in the Post-colonial Moment

DYMPNA CALLAGHAN

[Post-colonialism embraces a number of discourses and approaches to the literary text, but its prime concern is also to question the universal validity of master narratives from non-literary sources wherein the 'primitive' is depicted only so as to shore up the 'civilized' and the Western and so economically dominant sectors of the world economy pose as representative of 'global' concerns. This could comprise several methods, and so takes the application of its core interests and aims from a nexus of different, if still associated, concerns (deconstructive, feminist, cultural materialist). Most consistently, post-colonial writing has attempted to place on the map those who had hitherto been invisible within traditional historiography. In this, it shares the same concerns as feminist and Marxist revisions of the past, with this caveat: that these approaches may not directly include an awareness of how 'occidental' they really are. As Edward Said has traced in his essay, 'Traveling Theory' (Said 1984: 226–47), ideas do not remain intact and untranslatable if adopted in different cultural contexts. There is thus always a 'subaltern' tendency to subvert and *mis*understand the discourses of a different culture, and this is not error as typically understood, but a necessary resistance to white Anglo-Saxon Protestant cultural imperialism.

In the work of Gayatri Chakravorty Spivak issues of race, class and gender are interwoven: a deliberate variety of perspective is preferred to rationally and empirically derived deductions from what has been allowed to be recorded in the archive. In this, Spivak is nearest the strategies of deconstruction. Indeed, she introduced and translated Jacques Derrida's seminal work, *Of Grammatology*, in 1976, which (among many other matters) emphasized the relativity of all of our linguistic structures. Put at its most reductive, this is to remove all support from notions of the 'natural' or 'commonsensical' when we would have language point to the world. Instead of positive and stable items captured more or less closely in language, there is only ever 'difference' between terms – no ethical or God-given value that perennially weights certain terms with greater validity than others (for example, black/white, man/woman, East/West). All expression chases an identity with the real or original intention taken to lie behind the written. In so doing, it inevitably produces an excess of meaning, a 'supplement', that actually indicates both that the expressed sentiments are always lacking in full and self-sufficient meaning and that we create truths through the frames in which we arbitrarily package our apparent intentions. Meaning is constantly deferred:

> Through this sequence of supplements there emerges a law: that of an endless linked series, ineluctably multiplying the supplementary mediations that produce the sense of the very thing that they defer . . . Immediacy is derived. Everything begins with the intermediary . . .
>
> (Derrida 1976: 157)

That West and East are rather more states of mind than geographical locations informs Spivak's work throughout.

Dympna Callaghan does not here attempt to represent all the many possible strategies of reading that Spivak's work pursues, but rather concentrates on how interpretation of *Antony and Cleopatra* is deeply affected by what Spivak termed in a 1982 essay, 'The Politics of Interpretations' (in Spivak 1988: 118–33), namely its ideologies projected into what seem disconnected aesthetic effects. Basic to this investigation is an understanding of how even Marx's categories of class can fail to account for the local variations between cultures, and just as crucially omits the voices of women (especially those from the Third World), the 'ideologically excluded other' (Spivak 1988: 129). This politics of exclusion operates even within texts that would appear to be striving to establish as broad a base of inclusion as possible.

In order to trace the excluded 'subaltern consciousness', one does not simply expose the metaphysical apologies for imperialism, but also deconstructs the deep structures formed by it within us – both the rulers *and* ruled (see Spivak's essay, 'Subaltern Studies: Deconstructing Historiography', in Spivak 1988: 197–221; and her 'Speculations on Reading Marx', in Attridge *et al.* 1987: 30–62). To be truly liberating such a move should expound a theory of change: how political action might derive from theoretical confrontation rather than from notions of transition and also how it must be accompanied by changes in the sign-systems that keep repression in place and acceptable. Cleopatra's voice, often stigmatized as sirenic and off-limits, is actually an indication (for those who have ears to hear) of liberation for the Roman world as well as the Alexandrian. We have to be aware of *how* we get our information about her and why it is structured quite in the way it is.

As defined in the Concise Oxford Dictionary, the term 'subaltern', means not only '[o]f inferior rank', but also, in a technical sense derived from formal logic, 'particular, not universal'. There is an irony at work in the title Subaltern Studies given to the several collections of radical essays on Indian History, for, first, there is no inferiority implied in the choice to view history from the 'bottom up', and second, it was only the colonial administrator who was content to regard individual acts of 'insurgency' as unconnected criminal actions motivated by purely personal mendacity.

The work of Ranajit Guha has done much to redefine our view of colonialist historiography and also its semantics. In his Elementary Aspects of Peasant Insurgency in Colonial India (1983a) he analyses the colonialist need to depict revolutionary peasant activity as sporadic breaches of law and order. Causal explanations were sought for ready-made conclusions, an induced 'historical truth', which was really just an 'apology for law and order – the truth of the force by which the British had annexed the subcontinent' (Guha 1983a: 3; see also Guha's 'The Prose of Counter-Insurgency', in Guha 1983b: 1–42). Underpinning Guha's account is Antonio Gramsci's perception that there is no such thing as spontaneity in history. As Guha understands it, 'this is precisely where they err who fail to recognize the trace of consciousness in the apparently unstructured movements of the masses' (Guha 1983a: 5). While such opposition was (and continues elsewhere to be) a 'negative and inversive procedure', this does not 'put it outside the realm of politics' (Guha 1983a: 9). For Gramsci, in his 'History of the Subaltern Classes: Some Methodological Criteria' (1934–5; excerpts in Gramsci 1971: 52–4), the very term 'subaltern' (the original use of the term as taken up by Guha and contributors), designates those who do not enjoy the collectivity of class-consciousness. Their 'instrumentality' is still a historical force capable of definition.

This has an immediate application in the analysis of those literary texts that portray the exotic or 'Oriental', for it is precisely this submerged other 'voice' which needs amplifying, if such writing is to be given its fullest context, for not only do we listen to the repressed, we can also identify the 'staged' conceptual power of imperialism. In Gramsci's work, there was a significant distinction between the material 'rule' of a presiding power and the 'hegemony' of the active, and so dominant, social and cultural forces that keep it in place (see Williams 1977: 108–14; Said 1984: 168–72; and, for an influential application of Gramsci to subaltern studies, Asok Sen's 'Subaltern Studies: Capital, Class and Community', in Guha 1987: 203–35). In becoming canonical, it is often the case that literary texts are used for the dissemination of residual 'hegemonic' images.

As Viswanathan (1989) has demonstrated, it is specifically the study of literature, never free of a particular cultural situation, that, far from ignoring the marginal or heterodox, actually 'contains' it. Mental production has the capacity to have as material an effect on culture as the economic base. Spivak has recently suggested further opportunities for turning the colonial power relation upside-down when we realize that the writing of history may always be a strategy. A crisis in political authority accompanies a 'functional change in a sign system', which is a 'violent event' (Spivak 1988: 197), and not a gradual evolution towards more sophisticated and 'textual' perceptions: it bears directly on lived experience. The process of reading invoked by Spivak is a transactional one, where the critical sense is fortified by the need to question, and so displace, accepted systems of meaning, the stories of Antony and Cleopatra we have been encouraged to 'know' (see also Young 1990: 157–62). The elaboration of a text need not be, therefore, a wilful evasion of what seems 'there' in the words on the page, because those very words never signify innocently or autonomously. 'Elaboration', for Gramsci, meant ordering 'in a systematic, coherent and critical fashion one's own intuitions of life and the world, and to determine exactly what is to be understood by the word "systematic", so that it is not taken in the pedantic and academic sense [as a natural law, impervious to changes wrought by human agency]' (Gramsci 1971: 327; see also Said 1984: 169–72). A politically aware criticism thus sets the text against past *and present* perceptions of reality (which in any given culture are never unitary or consistent) so as to withstand and so analyse the particular strategies any writing performs (see Spivak's 'The Problem of Cultural Self-representation', in Spivak 1990: 50–58).

Cleopatra is not only excluded on the grounds of race from serious Roman consideration, but also as one of those unruly females who wield power, and so have to be put back in their place. For all its salutary substitutions of communal power for centralized obedience, a subaltern theoretical insurgency needs to be reminded of the ease with which women and their historical agency can be made to appear discontinuous and marginal. Moved from clan to clan, or family to family, there is a material reason why women might not be heard, over and above the usual patriarchal deafness. Cleopatra, to be heard, has to be represented as contrary and perverse. The trick of it is to realize that the same may also be true of Octavius Caesar.]

NIGEL WOOD

Introduction

Since political critics vehemently disavow the notion that we can see in Shakespeare's plays how certain human values persist from Shakespeare's day to our own, it seems, at least at first glance, odd if not perverse that those same critics should be so determined to juxtapose his plays with contemporary theory. If Shakespeare's plays do not represent transhistorical themes and enduring human values, how can we possibly claim that they have any connection with the present, let alone with that abstruse body of texts known as 'theory'? Indeed, the logic of common sense seems to militate against a connection between Shakespeare and theory to the degree that one might well think that the two can be conjoined only by some rather tortuous rhetorical gymnastics. We may even find ourselves nodding in agreement with Gary Taylor's ironic assertion:

> Everything is related to everything else. So everything is relevant to Shakespeare, and Shakespeare is relevant to everything. Shakespeare, the apex of the inverted pyramid of interpretation, is also the tip of a funnel through which the whole world can be poured.
>
> (Taylor 1989: 352)

Political readings of literature, however, are not about establishing either the universal relevance of Shakespeare or an identity between the ideas of our own time and those of an earlier era, but rather about showing the ideological underpinnings of both conventional connections *and* dissociation between the past and the present, that is, political criticism endeavours to point out the ideological investment of the status quo in securing Shakespeare as a locus of universal human values. Thus, if Shakespeare's plays can be shown to convey universal human truths, it can be argued also that there is something immutable about the social order, something that is not subject to political change. The world can then be shown to be good as it is, and as it should remain. In this way, Shakespeare has been used to support the dominant ideology, that is the set of ideas and cultural practices that help to reproduce the social order along its current lines. It is from this perspective that theory seems irrelevant to Shakespeare, and because this is the perspective of the dominant ideology (the conventional habit of mind of our era) it has come to seem like common sense. (The point, of course, is that 'common sense' is itself ideological rather than natural.) In contrast, when political criticism makes connections between contemporary ideas, such as theory, the aim is neither to suggest seamless continuity with the past nor to obscure its status as ideologically motivated intervention; on the contrary, political criticism insists on that status.

It may seem surprising to learn that the political nature of literary culture, especially drama, was far from occluded in Shakespeare's own day. For instance, Elizabethans and Jacobeans were in the habit of making overtly political connections between history and contemporary events. They used the past in order to interpret the present, not in some neutral or arbitrary way, but from specific political and religious positions. Analogy and allegory were the mechanisms through which they drew parallels and correspondences that would produce the past as a political commentary upon the present (see Callaghan 1989: 9–33). The material of *Antony and Cleopatra*, in particular, seemed to lend itself to the making of what might even be dangerous political connections. We know, for example, that Fulke Greville wrote a play on the topic but threw it in the fire on account of, as he digresses in his 'Life of Sidney', the fear of emulating '[m]any members in that creature [the play] (by the opinion of those few eyes which saw it) and so spreading a childish wantonnesse in them, apt enough to be construed or strained to a personating of vices in the present Governors . . .' (Greville 1870, 4: 155). Thus, in Shakespeare's *Antony and Cleopatra*, the politics of imperial Rome and the reign of Cleopatra were critically related to the burgeoning ideology of nationalism in early modern England, the humanist fascination with the exotic, and to the vexed question of female sovereignty, which had plagued the reign of the recently deceased monarch, Elizabeth I.[1] Up to now, political criticism has largely concerned itself with demonstrating the historical importance of these issues for Shakespeare's play.

Patrick Brantlinger, in his influential analysis of post-colonial cultural studies, *Crusoe's Footprints: Cultural Studies in Britain and America*, points out that the most fundamental characteristic of reading practices broadly termed theoretical or political in this field is the move beyond the text despite the debate and confusion about what such a 'beyond' might consist of (Brantlinger 1990: 15). Similarly, the editors of *The Empire Writes Back: Theory and Practice in Post-colonial Literatures* point out:

> The subversion of a canon is not simply a matter of replacing one set of texts with another. This would be radically to simplify what is implicit in the idea of canonicity itself. A canon is not a body of texts *per se*, but rather a set of reading practices (the enactment of innumerable individual and community assumptions, for example about genre, about literature, and even about writing). So the subversion of a canon involves the bringing to consciousness and articulation of these practices and institutions, and will result not only in the replacement of some texts by others, or the redeployment of some hierarchy of value within them, but equally crucially by the reconstruction of the so-called canonical texts through alternative reading practices.
>
> (Ashcroft *et al.* 1989: 189)

Post-colonial critics have made calls to 'open up' literary texts. Here, I want to extend this strategy of political reading – immanent in the text itself – by 'opening up' Shakespeare's play, especially the representation of Cleopatra, to Gayatri Chakravorty Spivak's essay, 'Can the

Subaltern Speak?' (in Nelson and Grossberg 1988: 271–313). Relating Shakespeare's depiction of the dusky queen of Egypt to an essay on the representation of Third World women is not as arbitrary as it might first appear. For while the English Renaissance was not a 'First World' culture in the sixteenth and seventeenth centuries before the classifications 'First' and 'Third' Worlds came into being, it is certainly so now. The dissemination and reproduction of Shakespeare in the present-day currents of transnational capitalism is overwhelmingly hegemonic – and First World. Thus the practice of reading Shakespeare is deeply enmeshed in the conflictive relation between the hierarchically organized geographical and conceptual zones of 'First' and 'Third' Worlds. The challenge Spivak presents, then, is that of registering the present geo-political situation in Shakespeare studies. The critical issue here is not whether it is relevant to juxtapose Shakespeare with contemporary power relations structured via the dynamic modality 'First/Third World'; rather the point is that a fully historicized Shakespeare studies recognizes that every encounter with Shakespeare is already structured by that modality. In this way, Spivak compels us to address how our critical discourses are both positioned within and reproduce the hegemonic.

I have chosen Spivak's essay because in it she asks what it means to represent any marginalized population and what the Third World means to the West. Spivak is particularly concerned with how women of colour were represented in British imperialism of the nineteenth century when white colonizers found it convenient to eroticize the exploitation and oppression of non-white women, and upon occasion, to claim that their role was to protect them; that is, to represent someone may be in their interests because they may be unable to represent themselves. Alternatively, in certain situations, particularly colonialist ones, representing the interests of subjugated populations may be a ruse by means of which the colonizer presents his own interests in the guise of a benign and humanitarian gesture. Indeed, in such circumstances, representing, or perhaps misrepresenting, the colonized Other may work to silence the other altogether. Equally problematic for Spivak, however, is the notion often held by Western academics that they have no responsibility for addressing themselves to the concerns of the Third World. Spivak argues that to address oneself to the problems of the marginalized is a far cry from usurping the voice of the oppressed.

Spivak is one of the foremost theorists of our day: she introduced Derrida to English-speaking readers almost 20 years ago when she translated *Of Grammatology* (1976). The interviews in one of her most recent books, *The Post-colonial Critic* (1990) show that she is very conscious of being the conspicuous and allegedly inscrutable Bengali –

her writings and lectures are notoriously opaque – the exotic in a sari, in the white-dominated Western academy. Thus her own investment in questions of representing women of colour is considerable. She is supremely conscious of being understood to represent Third World women, who, in contrast to her own privileged position, suffer the exploitation of multinational capitalism.

In applying 'Can the Subaltern Speak?' to *Antony and Cleopatra*, I will proceed by first explicating Spivak's essay and then by analysing the play from its perspective. I should point out from the start that I do not propose to 'apply' in a mechanistic way Spivak's theoretical ruminations on representation and the Third World to Shakespeare's *Antony and Cleopatra* as if there were some simple and straightforward correspondence between the two texts. Instead, I want to pursue some of the broader implications of Spivak's thinking for a critical interpretation of Cleopatra. My objective will be to read the politics of representation in the play in oblique relation to the problem of representing the raced and gendered Other outlined in Spivak's text.

Spivak's work is characterized by an insistence on forging connections between apparently antithetical bodies of theoretical work, namely Marxism, feminism, and deconstruction, theories which she uses to articulate the complex and often contradictory interrelations between gender, race and class in the post-colonial era. She writes: 'I am a *bricoleur*, I use what comes to hand' (in McRobbie 1985: 8). Her use of different bodies of theory is, however, rather less arbitrary than that statement might lead us to believe. Multiple theoretical discourses are always deployed in relation to a core concern, namely the relation between the West and its knowledges and the subjugated Third World. The relation between these (one can hardly think of a more intractable, problematic and all-encompassing relation), which is one both of connection and disjuncture, is the focus of Spivak's theoretical explorations. The absolute and excoriating division between the First World and the Third constitutes the structure of the now accelerated global expansion of capital. Multinational corporations exploit cheap labour in the Third World, making structural inequity vital to the existence of the First World itself.

Nothing could seem more alien to Shakespeare's *Antony and Cleopatra*. Once again, my purpose in juxtaposing these apparently incompatible categories is not to plead that Shakespeare studies is or should be causally or directly related – that is, 'relevant' in the pragmatic sense – to all social ills and economic inequities on a world scale, but rather that this juxtaposition helps 'to raise neglected questions about structures of domination and their links to modes of cultural production' (Thomas 1991: ix). It is precisely such questions that Spivak insistently addresses, showing that cultural production (especially literature, literary theory and criticism) are not somehow magically severed from the global organization of economic production. These are, then, precisely the conditions in which we read and interpret *Antony and Cleopatra*. Spivak insists that we recognize our geographical and political locatedness, that we become cognizant of the space from which we read. It is important to point out that locatedness is not the same as identity. We are not asked to reveal an essential identity as First World readers or to feel guilty, or to qualify our every utterance. Rather an objective articulation of our situatedness is required if we are not unconsciously and implicitly to endorse the status quo by behaving as if living in the West required no further comment. The politics of position is, of course, supremely relevant to *Antony and Cleopatra* because the play itself endlessly rehearses the problematics of positionality in numerous shifts of scene across the continents and in the fragmentation of Antony's status as tragic hero. When Antony is dead, Cleopatra resurrects the image of the heroic Antony who mastered through conquest the contradictions of a divided world:

> His legs bestrid the ocean; his reared arm
> Crested the world; his voice was propertied
> As all the tunèd spheres – and that to friends –
> But when he meant to quail and shake the orb,
> He was as rattling thunder. For his bounty,
> There was no winter in't – an autumn 'twas
> That grew the more by reaping. His delights
> Were dolphin-like; they showed his back above
> The elements they lived in. In his livery
> Walked crowns and crownets; realms and islands were
> As plates dropped from his pocket
>
> (V.ii.82–92)

Here, Antony becomes the hero who can stand astride the chasm between Rome and Egypt, not the disintegrated personality we have watched swallowed up by it. This is the myth of the tragic hero's coherence, and Cleopatra's articulation of it only serves to heighten the way that tragedy itself, its status as a genre, is so problematized by this play. Tragedy is one narrative frame by means of which we can impose order and sense on the way power is exerted in the world, and what is so fascinating about the play is the way it probes the inconsistencies of the narrative.

In a similar sense, we might say that Spivak's *bricolage* is an attempt at a theory of such inconsistencies and contradictions. Thus a political position for Spivak is a recognition of geo-political locatedness, but not a confinement to it or to any single theoretical apparatus. Spivak is not herself formulating a single theory but rather utilizing a body of theoretical knowledge – feminism, Marxism and Derridean deconstruction – to tackle that set of problems produced by the global division of labour.

Taking as my starting-point Spivak's interrogative, 'Can the subaltern speak?', I will argue that the raced and gendered Other is in a significant sense – in exactly the same sense that the subaltern is unrepresentable for Spivak – unrepresentable in *Antony and Cleopatra*.

The Subaltern Cannot Speak

For Spivak the connection between the fundamentally economic binarism, First/Third worlds, and the business of literary criticism, that is, the question of cultural production, lies in the concept of representation. This is because the asymmetrical relation between the First World and the Third, between the 'developed', capitalist West and the rest of the world, is secured by the fact that the First World has controlled the depiction of the Third World and has done so to its own advantage. Another way of saying this is that culture offers ideological ramification for the nature of this hierarchical relation (although it can also be a site of contestation). What is at issue, then, is how the Third World functions *as* a representation in and for the West. For Spivak, the question of representation is the pre-eminent predicament of the post-colonial condition – who speaks for whom, for Third World subjects, especially Third World women, and can they speak for themselves?

In order to grasp the significance of Spivak's essay in relation to the mechanisms of representation, it is first important to understand something of the resonance of the term within the history of Western thought. With the advent of post-structuralism, the problem of representation at the level of language is exacerbated by the demise of the long assumed correspondence between words and things, the signifier and the signified. Post-structuralist theory has shown that the relation between these two components of the sign is arbitrary and unstable. This move has its corollary in the political sphere at the level of democratic representation where the long-held Enlightenment assumption that the rights – and thence political representation – accorded to the privileged white male subject could be almost infinitely extended to include all social groups, has been challenged by the fact that such democratic inclusion was based on the fundamental identity of all subject groups with the paradigmatic, universal Western man. That is to say, claims for the rights of women and minorities were based on the degree to which those marginalized groups could prove their fundamental similarity with the paradigmatic subject, 'Man'. In other words, the argument for rights had to be something of the order of 'Underneath it all we are just like you'. Paradoxically, of course, Man was accorded his privileged status by defining himself against those he excluded (those who were not 'like him') and who now question the political usefulness of claiming the right to be represented on the grounds of a sameness which can only corroborate his hegemony. That is, 'Man' patently does not represent everyone, nor can he ever do so.

As in the relation between the signifier and the signified, the emphasis has turned from 'sameness', a relation of fundamental identity and symmetry, to one of difference and discontinuity. 'The ideological conjuncture of two crucial modes of understanding representation', 'speaking for' as in politics, and 're-presentation' as in art or philosophy, are for Spivak 'related but irreducibly discontinuous understandings of the word' (Nelson and Grossberg 1988: 275). One has only to look, as Virginia Woolf did in *A Room of One's Own* (1929; Woolf 1992), at the predominance of women as a preoccupation of literature despite their almost total absence as writing subjects to see why these two modes of representation are only loosely analogous. Representations at every level – linguistic and social – are not, therefore, neutral empirical records of objective reality, but interested constructions of it, whose function is either to challenge or secure hegemonic interests.

These, then, are the political and theoretical developments which inform the interrogative of Spivak's title, 'Can the Subaltern Speak?', which derives from Karl Marx's famous dictum in *The Eighteenth Brumaire of Napoleon Bonaparte* (1851–2): 'They [small peasant proprietors] cannot represent themselves; they must be represented' (Marx 1977: 318). Here, of course, Marx is not announcing a prohibition against the representation of the subaltern classes, but rather making an objective determination that such representation is impossible as a direct result of the material and ideological forces which preclude the peasant classes from knowledge of the nature of their own subordination.

The subaltern is a term which has become important in recent years in the work of a group of Indian historians, whose endeavours have taken the title 'subaltern studies'. Subaltern studies endeavours to recover the histories of those who have been denied both voice and record in Western history – that is, those who, because they are deprived of political representation, have all been effectively erased from the historical record. They are 'unrepresented' in both the social-democratic sense and the philosophical sense. The project of subaltern studies 'is to rethink Indian colonial historiography from the perspective of the discontinuous chain of peasant insurgencies during the colonial occupation' (Nelson and Grossberg 1988: 283). While this project is a laudable one – and Spivak is aware of the parallel project of feminist 'archaeology' whereby the history of Western women is uncovered beneath the patriarchal record (Nelson and Grossberg 1988: 287) – she remains critical of some of its assumptions: 'there is no unrepresentable subaltern subject that can know and speak itself' (Nelson and Grossberg 1988: 285). Unlike bourgeois Western women, for example, who can trace the history of their silencing, the marks of their suppression for themselves, the subaltern cannot undo her erasure. Thus for Spivak, intellectuals cannot abdicate the responsibility of representing those whose existence lies beyond the structures of representation: one cannot gain access to the allegedly pure peasant political consciousness posited by the subaltern group. However, she conceives this not as the necessity of speaking for the subaltern class but rather as *speaking to* the history of muted subalternity (Nelson and Grossberg 1988: 295).

Jaques Derrida, the post-structuralist theorist most closely associated with the crisis of the sign I have briefly delineated above, has been concerned with the linguistic and philosophical as opposed to the specifically political problem of representation. Yet Spivak argues that Derrida's deconstruction (the mechanism whereby difference is immanent in any instance of apparent identity), is of enormous political value because it is able to address 'the topographical reinscription of imperialism' (Nelson and Grossberg 1988: 290) inherent in the processes of representation. This claim directly counters the widely held notion that Derrida places too great an emphasis on 'textuality', precisely at the expense of real political issues. Spivak explains:

> I will discuss a few aspects of Derrida's work that retain a long-term usefulness for people outside the First World. This is not an apology. Derrida is hard to read; his real object of investigation is classical philosophy. Yet he is less dangerous when understood than the first-world (*sic*) intellectual masquerading as the absent nonrepresenter who lets the oppressed speak for themselves.
> (Nelson and Grossberg 1988: 292)

Derrida, then, does not pretend to the position of the intellectual who regards himself as invisible, completely absent from the systems he analyses. Nor does he absent himself from the responsibilities of having the power to represent:

> Derrida here makes . . . choices to suggest a critique of European ethnocentrism in the constitution of the Other. As a postcolonial intellectual, I am not troubled that he does not *lead* me (as Europeans inevitably seem to do) to the specific path that such a critique makes necessary. It is more important to me that, as a European philosopher, he articulates the *European* Subject's tendency to constitute the Other as marginal to ethnocentrism and locates *that* as the problem with all logocentric . . . endeavours . . . *Not* a general problem but a European problem.
>
> (Nelson and Grossberg 1988: 293)

Spivak's point here is that Derrida cannot be upbraided for having failed to apply his theories to the instance of the non-European subject because such an application would merely re-enact the process of Othering inherent in Western rationalism (logocentrism) that Derrida strives to deconstruct. Spivak continues: 'what I find useful is the sustained and developing work on the *mechanics* of the constitution of the Other; we can use it to much greater analytic and interventionist advantage than invocations of the *authenticity* of the Other' (Nelson and Grossberg 1988: 294). Investigating the 'mechanics' of Othering involves the West's production of the Other for itself rather than the relation that an already constituted Other has for the West: what is it about the West that requires an exotic and subjugated Other?

The feminist component of Spivak's analysis emerges when she urges that the problem of representing the subaltern is exacerbated in the instance of the female subaltern who is subject to the double mechanism of invisibility enjoined upon her by her racial status within the hierarchy of the British Empire and its legacy and by her gender. Spivak's essay ends with an analysis of the British condemnation and legal prohibition of suttee, the practice whereby widows immolate themselves on the funeral pyres of their husbands, and of the suicide of one of her own politically active female relatives. Spivak asks if these gruesome efforts can be read as instances in which the female subaltern has, against all the odds, succeeded in a mortal act of self-representation. She concludes that they cannot. At such extremity, the point where self-representation becomes possible only through an act of self-annihilation, the bloody trace of a self-representing subject is inscrutable, almost indecipherable.

Reading *Antony and Cleopatra* via 'Can the Subaltern Speak?'

I want now to use Spivak's essay to pose a fundamental question for

Shakespeare's *Antony and Cleopatra*: What does Cleopatra represent? Spivak's text allows us to ask whether Cleopatra can function as anything other than an exotic, racially marked heroine who is yet another manifestation of 'orientalism' (see Hughes-Hallett 1990: 365–79; Hamer 1993: 28–34). This term was coined by Edward Said to denote the discursive construction of an East whose status as an object of Western knowledge is premised on disallowing the present existence of its populations (Said 1978). The point here is not, of course, to suggest direct relations between Cleopatra, 'tawny' queen of ancient Egypt, and disempowered, unrepresented Third World women, but rather to demonstrate that an awareness of their existence may make us pose entirely different questions about Shakespeare's play. Instead of accepting the fiction of Cleopatra's status as a subject of representation, we can analyse her as an object of it – one which tells us not about femininity, Egyptian or otherwise, but about the Western masculinity which has fantasized her into existence.

Shakespeare's play is in a certain sense *about* the business of representing femininity, about simultaneously using and exploding stereotypes about women. Instead of using the usual Renaissance conventions for depicting woman in terms of the polar opposites, the virgin or the whore, the paragon of female obedience or the witch, Shakespeare presents us with a character whose very fascination lies in the curious admixture of these qualities. Neither chaste nor obedient, but powerful and sexual, this inversion of the usual order of sexual attraction seems to be premised on Cleopatra's status as the exotic woman, who abides not in the threatening proximity of domestic space but in the fascinating, sexually compelling and distant realm of the Other, of all that is not familiar and decidedly not reminiscent of home. Despite the title, the play is about how the enigmatic Cleopatra tipped the balance of power in the Roman Empire. There is no record of the play having been performed in Shakespeare's lifetime, and it may well be that the role was too taxing for a young male performer who would be required to simulate not just femininity, but overpowering, mature sexual allure.

Critical discussions of Cleopatra typically frame themselves in terms of potentially endless controversy about whether she is merely an alluring harlot, and whether she achieves genuinely tragic stature[2]. Even feminist critical interventions have not questioned the structure of this impasse but rather tend to argue that Cleopatra is a positive representation of female power (see Jankowski 1992: 146–82). There has been much reluctance about recognizing that as the West's fantasy of the East, Cleopatra achieves tragic stature because of her libidinous nature. Cleopatra's power is fundamentally histrionic, a matter of 'dramatic skill that enables her to control her world by controlling how others see her, through careful staging of her natural body to serve her political ends'. This power comes both from 'the character's skill in creating fictions and her ability to act them' (Jankowski 1992: 161). This is the means whereby 'Cleopatra unites her natural and political bodies to control an enemy – Rome – and maintain the sovereignty of her kingdom. They also reveal Cleopatra's astonishing ability to control through her own flexibility the shifting fortunes of a mutable universe' (Jankowski 1992: 161). For other critics, Cleopatra's dramatic talents are intrinsically manipulative and duplicitous, and are – paradoxically enough – the dramatic enactment of Renaissance antitheatricalism. All the evils of the theatre, the semblances of power which might entail its usurpation, could be figured forth in the boy actor playing the fickle Egyptian queen (see Singh 1989; Rackin 1972). Critics almost universally agree that 'Cleopatra is constantly in control of her world', so that the interpretative issue becomes not the status of her character as a representation but whether or not she exercises power well or badly (Jankowski 1992: 160).

The focus on Cleopatra's moral standing has also detracted from the geo-political issues in which she is embroiled. In fact, this play is quite unusual in the degree to which it insists on global dimensions, on the vast business of making history and politics, making connections between far-flung corners of the world as part of the single project of empire and the teleology of history. Antony and Cleopatra are not tragic lovers in splendid isolation, but personalities caught up in the transactions of Roman imperialism. In order to foreground this dimension of their relationship, the play pointedly violates the classical unities of time, place and action, with large numbers of scene changes – there are 16 scenes in Act IV, for instance – and switches from Rome to Alexandria and elsewhere that convey a sense that this is a drama of global proportions, one about the history of the world as a narrative of the conquest of its geography. Conquest and submission at the level of Roman imperialism has its parallel in the dynamics of domination and subjugation of the play's erotics.

It is striking that one of the preoccupations of the conquered Cleopatra of Act V of Shakespeare's play is with the representations and potential misrepresentations of her personage and her sovereignty. Famously, in one of the play's many self-reflexive or metatheatrical moments, she imagines her fate as theatrical spectacle in Rome before an audience – the lower orders of the imperial power – bearing an all too accurate resemblance to the throng at the Globe in its initial performances:

> Now, Iras, what think'st thou?
> Thou, an Egyptian puppet shall be shown
> In Rome as well as I. Mechanic slaves
> With greasy aprons, rules, and hammers shall
> Uplift us to the view. In their thick breaths,
> Rank of gross diet, shall we be enclouded,
> And forced to drink their vapour. . . .
> . . . Saucy lictors
> Will catch at us like strumpets, and scald rhymers
> Ballad us out o'tune. The quick comedians
> Extemporally will stage us, and present
> Our Alexandrian revels – Anthony
> Shall be brought drunken forth, and I shall see
> Some squeaking Cleopatra boy my greatness
> I'th' posture of a whore.
>
> (V.ii.207–21)

The populace, figured here in all their redolent corporeality, have been throughout the play shown to be taciturn in their affections and allegiances are understood specifically as spectators, as an audience, the recipients of politically produced spectacle. Paradoxically, the audience of the conquerors consists of 'slaves' in a way that complicates any simple construction of the vanquished tawny queen and history's victims. Rather, we are confronted with the problem of understanding the business of history, who makes it and for whom, and of 'a heterogeneous field that problematizes the general notion of an undifferentiated colonial subject or subaltern – as indeed of a monolithic colonizing power' (Nelson and Grossberg 1988: 298). The 'shouting plebeians' have been the source of an earlier taunt from Antony, too (IV.xiii.34). It is not, then, simply the fact of public humiliation that is feared but rather the masses themselves, 'the shouting varletry/Of censuring Rome' (V.ii.56–7). The 'common body' (I.iv.44, according to Caesar), 'Our slippery people' (I.ii.184, according to Antony), so frequently referred to in the play is fickle, vacillating and raucous – in fact not terribly unlike the histrionic Cleopatra herself. The point here is that spectacle is intrinsically neither good nor bad. What is at issue is who controls, and throughout the play, the sense is that it is not really the triumvirs or Cleopatra who finally control performance but the spectators of Rome, the volatile mass who are contrasted to the relatively docile mobs of Egypt who come out to witness Cleopatra's splendid displays.

Importantly, Cleopatra is not alone in her concern about the

makings of history. Caesar, too, who has earlier been threatened by
Pompey's capacity to sway the masses, is concerned about how his
action will be presented for posterity. When he learns of Antony's
death he asks Proculeius:

> Go with me to my tent, where you shall see
> How hardly I was drawn into this war,
> How calm and gentle I proceeded still
> In all my writings. Go with me, and see
> What I can show in this.

(V.i.73–7)

Antony and Cleopatra thus articulates the problem of representation,
one of performance, reading and interpretation as the mechanisms
through which history is constituted. Power is seen to reside in an
audience, quite literally a crowd of spectators in Cleopatra's first envi-
sioning of her likely fate at Roman hands, and metaphorically, in the
second instance when Proculeius is made to participate as audience.
This is a cold and private form of display, far less vulnerable to the
reaction of the mob, but nevertheless one that seeks authorization
outside itself and makes Proculeius the synecdoche of posterity. This
might be said to be the play's fantasy of itself. Like the transparent
intellectual castigated by Spivak who refuses to recognize his own
positionality, the ideological project of the play admits no responsibility for its own capacity to control representation but allows it all
to devolve on to the spectator.

Female sovereignty, too, becomes effective through representation,
just as it did in Elizabeth's reign in royal progresses and officially sanc-
tioned portraits (see Berry 1989: esp. 83–110). In its explicitly theatrical
rendition, however (that is, histrionics confined within the institution
of theatre itself), mechanisms of display are revealed as constructions,
and possibly obfuscations of real power relations. So it is that while, at
one level, Cleopatra is presented as the exotic object of our gaze, and
yet at the moments she is most fully this, for example in Enobarbus's
famous barge speech, we do not see her at all; she exists only as representation, not as dramatic presence. Enobarbus, who is elsewhere the rank
misogynist, is susceptible to the seductions of female display:

> I will tell you:
> The barge she sat in, like a burnished throne
> Burned on the water; the poop was beaten gold,
> Purple the sails, and so perfumed that
> The winds were lovesick with them; the oars were silver,
> Which to the tune of flutes kept stroke, and made

The water which they beat to follow faster,
As amorous of their strokes. For her own person,
It beggared all description: she did lie
In her pavilion – cloth-of-gold tissue –
O'er-picturing that Venus where we see
The fancy out-work nature; on each side her
Stood pretty, dimpled boys, like smiling Cupids,
With divers-coloured fans, whose wind did seem
To glow the delicate cheeks which they did cool,
And what they undid did.

(II.ii.197–212)

Cleopatra manufactures a sumptuous spectacle, but also an explicitly erotic one, with which Antony sitting on his throne in the marketplace in a vain endeavour to establish an alternative Roman power, cannot compete:

and Anthony,
Enthroned i'th'market-place, did sit alone,
Whistling to th'air, which but for vacancy
Had gone to gaze on Cleopatra too,
And made a gap in Nature.

(II.ii.221–5)

For want of an audience, Antony's enthronement is nothing but an empty gesture enacted in a vacuum. Cleopatra's display, in contrast, is usually read as enforcing her power, even if that power is defined in purely sexual terms. It is perhaps no coincidence that it is Enobarbus who finds this display so appealing – it verges in fact on the pornographic. The supine Cleopatra is, figuratively speaking at least, flagellated with silver oars, while flutes 'kept stroke' and the water itself is imaged as subject to sexual arousal by the action of the oars (II.ii.201–4). Cleopatra has 'o'er-pictured' Venus, the epitome of classical erotic representations of the female body and has 'made a gap in Nature'.

Having narrated with considerable skill the tale of Cleopatra's sexual self-representation (which we are given to believe is a tale passed on from man to man, 'if report be square to her' (II.ii.191–2, according to Mecenas); 'my reporter devised well for her' (II.ii.196, according to Agrippa)), Enobarbus goes on to describe the barge's female crew who are likened to the Nereides:

At the helm
A seeming mermaid steers; the silken tackle

Swell with the touches of those flower-soft hands
That yarely frame the office.

(II.ii.215–18)

The image of female sailors handling tackle is transmuted into a specifically sexual caress that brings the phallic member to the point of tumescence.

Representations are not 'natural'; they are rather erotic stagings which invariably have a feminine inflection even when Antony rather than Cleopatra is their subject. Antony enquires of Eros:

Wouldst thou be windowed in great Rome, and see
Thy master thus with pleached arms, bending down
His corrigible neck, his face subdued
To penetrative shame, whilst the wheeled seat
Of fortunate Caesar, drawn before him, branded
His baseness that ensued?

(IV.xv.72–7)

The Roman spectacle entails specifically sexual postures of domination and submission, as for instance in the 'penetrative shame' perpetrated on Antony by the riding Caesar. Conventional gender and power prerogatives are reversed:

Let him for ever go – let him not, Charmian!
Though he be painted one way like a Gorgon,
The other way's a Mars.

(II.v.116–18)

Antony becomes for Cleopatra the castrating gaze of the gorgon as much as the representative of Roman valour, and crucially he also becomes a *representation* and thereby subject to the feminine process of being 'painted' – cosmeticized. What Antony represents, his identity, and his role in Roman imperialism become radically unstable even at the moment when he has broken the effeminizing fetters of Egypt for the phallic duties of Rome. Antony's problem has always been one of 'going native', becoming like the terrain he ostensibly conquers, though elsewhere it has served him well:

thou once
Was beaten from Modena, where thou slew'st
Hirtius and Pansa, consuls, at thy heel
Did Famine follow, whom thou fought'st against –
Though daintily brought up – with patience more,
Than savages could suffer. Thou didst drink

The stale of horses, and the gilded puddle
Which beasts would cough at. Thy palate then did deign
The roughest berry and the rudest hedge.
Yea, like the stag, when snow the pasture sheets,
The barks of trees thou browsed. On the Alps
It is reported thou didst eat strange flesh,
Which some did die to look on.

(I.iv.56–68)

Antony's tendency is not to project the Other, but to become it. In this sense, Antony has served as the sort of subjectivity required in expanding the boundaries of empire. Cannibalism, drinking urine and living like one who has never known the niceties of Roman civilization proves Antony's masculinity, his ability to soldier in the service of Rome. Antony has merely reverted here by force of circumstances to the 'natural' state, rude and barbaric. In Egypt, in contrast, he has become 'voluptuous', a condition which rather than being the antithesis of civilization is a feminine counterpoint to it.

Antony has luxuriated in Egypt to the point of literally making a spectacle of himself, 'in the public eye', 'I'th' common show-place' (III.vi.11–12) with Cleopatra and their progeny. This display is not the rigorously controlled victory march but a decadent spectacle of excess for its own sake:

I'th'market-place on a tribunal silvered,
Cleopatra and himself in chairs of gold
Where publicly enthroned; at the feet sat
Caesarion, whom they call my father's son,
And all the unlawful issue that their lust
Since then hath made between them. Unto her
He gave the stablishment of Egypt, made her
Of lower Syria, Cyprus, Lydia,
Absolute queen.

(III.vi.3–11)

The object of Roman display is to consolidate power, not to abdicate it as Antony has done, and legitimize the progeny of an illicit relationship with a woman he has ostensibly conquered.

Despite the fact that Antony has become the feminized object of display, the tragic conclusion hinges crucially not on the death of Antony, but the fate of Cleopatra. This is because it is only Cleopatra who can serve fully as erotic spectacle once Antony has regained (as he does in Act IV) the masculinity required for the death of a male tragic protagonist. Antony is dispatched in Act IV so that the stage is left open for complete focus on the death of Cleopatra. The rationale for this at the level of the operations of the plot is that Caesar needs Cleopatra kept alive so that he can lead her in the triumph. She, of course, cunningly thwarts his ends. Earlier in the play, Cleopatra's 'dying' at the prospect of Antony's departure has been the butt of Enobarbus's obscene jokes:

ENOBARBUS: What's your pleasure, sir?
ANTHONY: I must with haste from hence.
ENOBARBUS: Why then, we kill all our women. We see
    how mortal an unkindness is to them: if they suffer our
    departure death's the word.
ANTHONY: I must be gone.
ENOBARBUS: Under a compelling occasion let women die. It
    were pity to cast them away for nothing – though
    between them and a great cause, they should be esteemed
    nothing. Cleopatra catching but the least noise of this,
    dies instantly – I have seen her die twenty times upon far
    poorer moment. I do think there is mettle in death,
    which commits some loving act upon her, she hath such a
    celerity in dying. . . . We cannot call her winds and
    waters sighs and tears: they are greater storms and
    tempests than almanacs can report . . . she makes a shower
    of rain as well as Jove.
                                    (I.ii.131–43, 146–8, 149–50)

Enobarbus puns on the histrionics of death and (feigned) female orgasm. Female sexual ecstasy (and indeed femininity itself) are fundamentally matters of theatrical representation. Whether death with the asp makes Cleopatra noble or whether her death is merely another, albeit extreme, rendition of the overblown behaviour described by Enobarbus has been the source of much critical debate: is she indeed a beguiling whore who paltered with Caesar, or a woman 'marble constant'? As a tragic denouement the asp scene is an odd one. A clown ready with misogynist rhetoric bears the asp to Cleopatra, and she is left with a mark of death that connotes the female genital aperture: 'There is a vent of blood, and something blown – The like is on her arm' (V.ii.347–8). The representation of Cleopatra as a projection of the sexually dominating, exotic woman comes to a crisis at the moment of tragic denouement and the play leaves us pondering femininity as itself the disquieting mark of something that is not there.

The Impossibilities of Representation

So far, we have considered Cleopatra from the general standpoint of Western systems of representation addressed by Spivak. But it is probably not inappropriate now to make a more direct parallel. For the problem of reading, the interpretative problem invariably posed by suicide is one taken up quite explicitly by Spivak, first in the ritualized instance of suttee and later in the case of the suicide of a young woman to whom Spivak is related.

There appear to be only two possible ways of reading suttee, both unsatisfactory: indigenous valorization of the practice and colonial condemnation of it. (A satisfactory representation would, of course, require some articulation of the victim's perspective.) The British, of course, sought to prevent suttee, but their reasons for doing so emanated in no sense from a commitment to the female subaltern's autonomy. Rather, the position of the British in India on suttee was that of 'white men saving brown women from brown men'. Spivak writes:

> Obviously I am not advocating the killing of widows. I am suggesting that, within the two contending versions of freedom, the constitution of the female subject in life is the place of the *différend*. In the case of the widow self-immolation, ritual is not being redefined as superstition but as *crime*. The gravity of suttee was that it was ideologically cathected as 'reward', just as the gravity of imperialism was that it was ideologically cathected as 'social mission'.
>
> (Nelson and Grossberg 1988: 301)

Thus, the unrepresentable woman is not simply left alone and left out, but victimized by the systems of representation which violently exclude her. This is the consequence, Spivak argues, of the fact that '[b]etween patriarchy and imperialism, subject-constitution and object-formation, the figure of the woman disappears, not into a pristine nothingness, but into a violent shuttling which is the displaced figuration of the third-world woman' (Nelson and Grossberg 1988: 306).

The historical record is monopolized by petty bureaucrats of the raj, and the victims of suttee remain the eroticized, mistranscribed and mistranslated names of the victims used by the British as evidence of the barbarity of Hindu law defined by them as 'a system which looked only for prettiness and constancy in woman': 'Ray Queen, Sun Ray, Love's Delight, Garland, Virtue Found, Echo, Soft Eye, Comfort, Moonbeam, Love-lorn, Dear heart, Eye-play, Arbour-born, Smile,

Love-bud, Glad Omen, Mist-clad, or Cloud-sprung' (Nelson and Grossberg 1988: 305). Spivak sharply reminds us that '[t]here is no more dangerous pastime than transposing proper names into common nouns, translating them, and using them as sociological evidence' (Nelson and Grossberg 1988: 306). Spivak is correct in saying that there can be no authentic representation of the Other by the West, and that even if the subaltern could speak for herself her speech would not necessarily be liberatory or represent her 'true interests'. However, what she does not allow for is that even blatant misrepresentation, as in the egregious instances of mistranslated, mistranscribed and misinterpreted nomenclature above, leaves a trace and connotes a subject whose absence then becomes visible at least (see Alcoff 1991–2, 7–22).

The final example of this phenomenon Spivak offers us is that of a young girl who hanged herself in 1926 but who had waited for the onset of menstruation in order that her death not be misread as a case of illicit love which had resulted in pregnancy. In fact, Spivak assures us, the cause of her suicide was a result of being asked to commit an assassination by fellow-activists in the struggle for Indian independence. The history of the Third World and the Third World woman's struggle to represent herself remains, then, enigmatic and impossible. Even women, and intellectual women, perpetuate the non-representation of the female subaltern:

> I know of Bhuvaneswari's life and death through family connections. Before investigating them more thoroughly, I asked a Bengali woman, a philosopher and Sanskritist whose early intellectual production is almost identical to mine, to start the process. Two responses: (a) Why, when her two sisters, Saieswari and Raseswari, led such full and wonderful lives, are you interested in the hapless Bhuvaneswari? (b) I asked her nieces. It appears that it was a case of illicit love.

The responsibility, as Spivak puts it, of the feminist critic cannot be that of putting the record straight, however; simply filling in the gaps. Rather, her task is to show that the very structure of cultural representations is predicated upon certain systematic exclusions. As feminist critics of Shakespeare, it is not our task to represent Cleopatra well despite the misogyny of her critical antagonists. It is all too easy to succumb to the temptation to find in Shakespeare's depiction of Egypt's 'tawny' queen a place where we can celebrate the representation of non-Western femininity, and a very powerful femininity at that. In Shakespeare's play we do not have access to powerful, racially marked femininity, but only to the mechanisms of theatrical representation itself. *Antony and Cleopatra* is an important cultural document in the history of the West's eroticization, and thence subjugation, of the raced woman as Other, a complex male fantasy and projection.[3] Indeed, it is because the Other is always a projection, a complex and culturally necessary fantasy, that Cleopatra cannot represent authentic alterity. The point is not so much that Cleopatra is misrepresented within the Western frame of the signifying subject and signified Other, but that the Other she purports to represent is beyond that system of representation. For the voice Cleopatra is given, hubristic and voluble though it is, is merely an instance of elaborate Western ventriloquism.

Thus, the feminist task of interpretation cannot simply be one of drawing attention to the long critically suppressed marks of Cleopatra's power or blackness – that is, to say, here we have over-looked and sometimes whitened an image of black femininity in canonical literature – even though that is an important and necessary empirical recognition.

The political limitations of such a position are fairly obvious: it can easily be appropriated to the reactionary notion that Shakespeare did indeed represent every conceivable aspect of humanity and that he is truly timeless, having even anticipated the interest in the 'theme' of women of colour in literature. It is a more complex and more urgent task to show that even in the process of ostensibly being represented, the category of radical female alterity is absent as ever, its representation barred by a cunning simulation. As Spivak puts it: 'These considerations would revise every detail of judgement that seem valid for a history of the West' (Nelson and Grossberg 1988: 306). By engaging in such a critique we cannot speak for the female subaltern but we can begin to change those discursive conditions within which her silence is produced and perpetuated.

SUPPLEMENT

NIGEL WOOD: In your *Woman and Gender in Renaissance Tragedy* (1989), you challenge the patriarchal structures of traditional tragic themes and also suggest how a political feminism might claim the genre as a site of necessary transgression. Is there the possibility that tragedy might be founded on a less repressive paradigm?

DYMPNA CALLAGHAN: Yes, I think it is possible, but I don't know that we at this historical juncture would recognize it as tragedy. Ibsen's *Doll's House* (1879), of course, sought to show that femininity epitomizes the trapped and tragic state of being human, and it really placed female transgression centre-stage, which *Antony and Cleopatra* also does. I don't know, I find it hard to imagine a world where we wouldn't have to transgress. Perhaps we could have a tragedy based on ineradicable evil rather than on evil that naturalizes itself as destiny but which is really the product of our social frameworks.

NW: How do you regard Caesar's closing speech, where he presumably performs a choric function in praising the lovers quite at variance with a consistency of characterization? Couldn't he be regarded as endorsing the Otherness that the rest of the narrative undercuts?

DC: Caesar praises the lovers, but I don't see this as endorsing Otherness. I see it precisely as choric, formulaic, an element of the genre. Also, the speech is phenomenally self-aggrandizing, full of imperialist triumph:

> No grave upon the earth shall clip in it
> A pair so famous. High events as these
> Strike those that make them; and their story is
> No less in pity than his glory which
> Brought them to be lamented.
>
> (V.ii.357–61)

Caesar's glory, then, is dependent upon the pity the lovers' deaths produce. Now, Antony and Cleopatra, instead of being a drunk and a whore who have brought ruin on themselves become the noble lovers vanquished by the great Caesar. Antony and Cleopatra are noble only to the degree that they embellish Caesar's honour. This seems like a fairly standard ruse of imperialism. Perhaps what is most interesting about it is that the internal conflicts of the rulers from Rome get finally and fully displaced on to problems at the periphery. What the lovers represent has been cut out of the heart of Empire itself.

NW: You pose the inevitability on p. 48 that Spivak's 'theory' comprises politically motivated *bricolage*. I'd like you to extend this perception not only to *Antony* but also to other plays in the canon. How can we identify the Other (oriental or not) in plays such as *Hamlet* or *Macbeth*? Do we regard Ophelia or Lady Macbeth's cries of anguish merely as madness? As these plays obey a specious ideological coherence, we obviously need to recategorize 'madness' and sanity – in criticism as well as our renditions of the play.

DC: We can identify the Other in other plays, of course, but the distinction between non-oriental and oriental forms of Otherness is crucial. It is really a matter of not conflating race and gender. I don't feel we can use racialized difference as a template that applies as much to *Hamlet* as to *Antony and Cleopatra*. The Otherness of *Hamlet* and *Macbeth* is in both instances constituted by women and the spectral, that is the apparitions which become feminized, which demand by their nature – especially in its dramatic rendition – to be looked at, opened to the gaze. These ghostly presences bring with them the authority of the other world, but they are, like women, unable to act directly. They can warn, curse and prophesy, those modes of speech most closely associated with femininity, but they cannot act directly on their own behalf. From the beginning of

Macbeth, we know that Lady Macbeth can't murder Duncan because of quintessentially feminine feeling, the role of a daughter, even though she claims she could set aside her maternal instincts when she begins to goad Macbeth to the murder. Ophelia, on the other hand is like a ghost even when she's alive. That's why, perhaps, one always thinks of her as a Pre-Raphaelite corpse. This is the Otherness of the gendered world and the Otherness of the supernatural, but it is not equivalent to racial difference, which demands different codes of dramatic representation. Nevertheless, I think you are right to suggest that all difference gets feminized to some extent, though I'd still maintain that this does not make race equivalent to femininity. In the figure of Cleopatra this becomes clear because she is so far from being deprived of agency, which is the predicament of the typical female character and the typical ghost. She can intervene – she does, however one wants to interpret her intervention, at Actium.

NW: The 'female' in *Antony and Cleopatra* is not at all comprehended by just the semiotics that surrounds Cleopatra. *Why* is Octavia so mute? Are Charmian, Iras and Alexas just aspects of Alexandria, that is, part of the metonymies that construct 'Egypt', or do they have separate work to do – either ideological or emancipatory – as part of the redefinition of the work of which they are a narrative item?

DC: I chose to concentrate on Cleopatra because I feel that all the questions about femininity – traditionally defined as not having access to power – emanate from her. I think we certainly see femininity de-essentialized in the play by being incorporated so much into Antony's persona. Octavia is silent because she is virtuous, and therefore literally partakes of masculine virtue. Of course, she's also something of the warrior. The reason for this is, I think, that the ideological work of delineating masculinity and femininity gets skewed by the pressure to differentiate the imperial from the colonized. In one way Cleopatra is such an unusual character precisely because the issue she forces upon the audience is one of power, not a problem of gender. The eunuch is a particularly interesting figure in this respect because he figures as what an indigenous Antony might have looked like – masculinity without the power. Charmian and Alexas, on the other hand, are examples of indigenous femininity without the power.

CHAPTER 3

Reading *Antony and Cleopatra*
through Irigaray's *Speculum*

MARY HAMER

[Mary Hamer's reading of *Antony and Cleopatra* explores just what might happen if we were to refuse to regard Cleopatra as a failed Roman. This attempt to escape ingrained and habitual structures of thought affects not just simply political responses to writing, but also the basis for all stereotyping, most crucially notions of the 'essential female'. The infinite variety of Cleopatra could, therefore, emerge as the necessary ingredient in 'Roman' thought that helps establish the male world as stable and perennial, progressive and purposive rather than yielding and passive. According to Luce Irigaray, what patriarchal language has left us with is a void when we come to try to locate women and their experiences outside masculinist parameters. In her *Speculum of the Other Woman* (1974; Irigaray 1985a), and *This Sex Which Is Not One* (1977; Irigaray 1985b), Irigaray explores with kaleidoscopic variety (that deliberately eschews the striving for regularity of grand theory) the possibility of new gynocentric voices. Even the term 'gynocentric' encourages the reduction of Irigaray's procedures to a repetitiveness true of the search for some essential characteristics.

Speculum takes its title from the curved mirror used in a woman's intimate self-examination. This mirror, folded back on itself, stands distinct from the more common flat mirror which opens on to a public gaze that replicates male-centred relations. Its curve ensures the only method of seeing the full anatomy of a woman's body, and, on a symbolic plane, thus of the existence of specific contours of her own (non-constructed, female) site of sexual difference. A direct gaze is not possible. In this, Irigaray takes issue with Freudian psychoanalysis, especially its view of female sexuality as the experience of a lack, the notorious references by Freud to a woman's 'penis envy', whereby girls sense an inferiority in that they do not possess the signifier of sexual potency, which in turn produces jealousy and a disavowal of their own sexual desires located in the body. As Freud termed it in his 1925 essay, 'Some Psychical Consequences of the Anatomical Distinction between the Sexes', girls may be driven to adopt male roles, and, further, develop a contempt for femininity:

> When she has passed beyond her first attempt at explaining her lack of a penis as being a punishment personal to herself and has realized that that sexual character is a universal one, she begins to share the contempt felt by men for a sex which is the lesser in so important a respect, and, at least in holding that opinion, insists on being like a man.
>
> (Freud 1953–74, 19: 253)

Irigaray takes radical issue with this patriarchal scientism. This 'phallocentric' prejudice against the poetic and inclusive (as opposed to goal-centred focus) necessarily fails to take account of significant psychosexual *and physical* differences between the sexes (see Irigaray 1985a: 55–61; Brennan 1992: 44–82).

Irigaray thereby celebrates fluidity and polysemy, which can dissolve forms ('Here is my space./Kingdoms are clay' (*Antony and Cleopatra*, I.i.36–7)) or offer alternatives to phallic power ('She made great Caesar lay his sword to bed./He ploughed her, and she cropped' (II.ii.234–5)). Female sexuality always evades the definitions of masculinity. In *This Sex Which Is Not One*, she even denies the female a role in traditional psychoanalytic terms. In this sense, it may not even be a 'sex' at all. A woman's syntax does not recognize 'either subject or object, "oneness" would no longer be proper meaning, proper names, proper attributes' (Irigaray 1985b: 134). Consequently, Cleopatra's denial of the simple mirroring of male, 'Roman', attitudes creates a necessary space for the exploration of interpretative and other freedoms, that are not held captive by the 'Visible', both physically and symbolically speaking. The result is an implicit ironizing of all attempts at clarity of discourse: woman's language 'never ends, it is powerful and powerless through its resistance to that which can be counted, it takes its pleasure and suffers through its hypersensitivity to pressure' – not possession (Irigaray 1985b: 110; see also Moi 1985: 138–43; Irigaray's, 'The Power of Discourse and the Subordination of the Feminine', in Whitford 1991: 118–32; and Kadiatu Kanneh's, 'Love, Mourning and Metaphor: Terms of Identity', in Armstrong 1992: 135–53). Cleopatra not only resists Roman possession, but our own critical appropriation.]

NIGEL WOOD

'Why, did he marry Fulvia and not love her?' (I.i.43). Cleopatra's question is too naïve for anyone who has been brought up in the Roman tradition to ask, no matter whether speaking on stage or listening from the audience. It takes a woman from outside the system to see the blank at its centre. Luce Irigaray, the Paris-based philosopher and psychoanalyst, bravely took the path of Cleopatra in 1974, when she published her book *Speculum of the Other Woman* (Irigaray 1985a). What, she asked, was going on in the famous texts by men that grounded the disciplines of philosophy and psychoanalysis? Look, she said, at how Freud and Plato use the figure of woman in their writing.[1] What is the part that the notion of woman is being made to play in grounding the masculine intellectual tradition, the ordering and interpretation of human life, produced and authorized by Western men? Romans, ancient and modern, know better than to ask such questions.

Irigaray was an outsider to the tradition she questioned only inasmuch as she was a woman; her Basque surname came from a husband. Born in Belgium, she had been trained at two universities, Louvain and Paris, in the disciplines of philosophy, linguistics, psychology and psychoanalysis. It was her doctoral thesis that she published under the title of *Speculum of the Other Woman*. In it she brought into question two of the most privileged texts in the system of knowledge in which she had been educated herself. As a woman, though, she had learned that a special place had been assigned to her within this system. She was not to share the position meant for men: I am not speaking now about jobs, though that will come into it in a moment. Sometimes it is claimed that when the terms 'man' or 'men' are used, both sexes are by implication included. Luce Irigaray had registered that the term 'woman' served a special function in authoritative texts which was not one served by the term 'man'. Setting herself to explore this function and to question it, she concluded that the figure of 'woman' – that is, the notion of some essential female – was not derived from any experience of living women, it was not a description. Rather it was a fantasy that Western men habitually used to fabricate a base for themselves, a stable ground on which to erect their accounts of human life. The 'knowledge' produced in this way, Irigaray proposed, perpetuated fantasies about men, too, fantasies that flattered their longing for wholeness and stability. No form of knowledge, she claimed, had been exempted from this governing principle. For her pains, on the publication of her book she was expelled from the élite École de Vincennes, the group of radical psychoanalysts that the famous reinterpreter of Freud, Jacques Lacan, had gathered about himself.

Irigaray's critical examination of the Western intellectual tradition begins by rereading Freud and works back in a historical sequence to

Plato. Her method is to put the tradition into question by reviewing its most privileged texts and reading them against the accepted grain, reading them, as one might say, otherwise. She takes Freud's own account of the way masculine identity is constructed and turns it round to ask what are its implications for women. What is to protect and insure this male 'I', once it is developed, how can it be reassured of its value? By taking this step, she brings her readers to a place where they can start to share the vision she has developed. Freud was a humanist, trying to put together a narrative of the single human psyche while never losing sight of the need to relate that story to the story of history, the ordering and understanding of public life that we call civilization. The male 'I' is proposed by Freud as the unit in civilization: an 'I' has to be developed in order for a moral sense to be exercised.[2] Before the development of the 'I', only drives exist, with no sense of responsibility outside the self. It is at this point in Freud's argument that Irigaray steps in. What provision is there, she asks, for the safety of this crucial structure, the single cell out of which the Western order is built?

She has taken Freud at his word and it brings her to a question that cannot easily be set aside. The answer she proposes is remarkable in its simplicity. The civilization that is grounded in the moral sense of the male depends for its continuance on the preservation of the male 'I', and it is the function of the female to safeguard that 'I'. It is more than 60 years since Virginia Woolf joked in *A Room of One's Own* (1929; Woolf 1992) that women had had the magic property of reflecting men at twice their natural size: in 1974 Luce Irigaray began enigmatically to expound that mirroring.

It was not just a question of propping up one man at a time, providing an enhanced sense of self-worth, through confirmation and approval. The critical act in this service exacted from women as a group is their suppression of difference. For the mirroring to work, that is, for it to support the male 'I' unconditionally, the woman must only reflect the image offered by the man, give him back what he already knows about himself. The notion is not difficult, almost embarrassingly obvious so far. But see what follows on conceding this. It means that in so far as women are different from men that difference is suppressed and excluded, hidden from male eyes and male knowledge.

This only matters if women are not exactly the same as men. Perhaps they are the same in some ways, you may object. Quite. But male knowledge, oddly enough, insists that women are very different from men, quite apart from that unfortunate matter of the defective part, the missing penis.[3] There is a problem here, about where the materials to construct this different kind of human person are to be found, in a world where only reflections of the male are permitted. Could it be that the qualities of its own that make the male 'I' feel precarious, so that it cannot tolerate recognizing them in itself and refuses to have them mirrored back, offer the stuff from which a 'woman-according-to-civilization' can be fabricated? Out of the rejected residue of the masculine, says Irigaray (1985a: 21–2), the notional feminine has been made up.

This leaves us all living in a world, Irigaray (1985a: 71) explains, where there is no knowledge of the female, only accounts of the male and its antithesis. Even this limited knowledge, Irigaray points out, is based on an idealized version of masculinity, one that defines itself as stable and completely integrated, not prone to change over time or riven by inner contradiction. It is a version of subjectivity that runs completely counter to what psychoanalysis teaches us about the shifting and contradictory impulses that make up our experience of ourselves. Yet this fiction of masculinity, she claims, is the fixed term around which human knowledge is organized. Freud, for example, when he set out to describe human sexuality, represented it as organized around the phallus: it seemed natural to him to arrange the evidence after that pattern. It is constantly repeated, producing, in Irigaray's words, a human world that functions as an economy of the same, where difference, objections or challenge to this endless repetition of the narrow same are not encountered.

Another term she has coined for this world is the *hommosocial economy*.[4] As she has argued, it is a world that neither knows nor acknowledges the reality of living women. It is created by men for their own use. Its affairs take place between men who subscribe to a common notion of what constitutes their masculinity: no disruption of this order is tolerated. In this economy the representation of women, though not the agency or subjectivity of actual women, does have an important part to play. 'Woman', the notion of some feminine essence, is the term on which the arrangements, pacts and narratives of the hommosocial world are founded.

But what about real women? They do exist. How do they know themselves? Only, she suggests, by refusing the part allotted to their sex in the Western intellectual tradition, by rejecting the chance to star as some mystical feminine and finding their own voices. If they were to speak for themselves they would utterly disrupt the monotonous repetition of the same. And only by speaking can they discover for themselves what is the nature of their desire. I was going to write 'discover for themselves and for civilization' but I held my hand.

Irigaray does not believe that civilization or patriarchy, as its excluded have come to call it, could survive hearing what women's voices, once raised, would bring into the human conversation. It would involve transformation.

It is patriarchal ways of knowing, the intellectual tradition, that an authentic knowledge of women would throw into disarray. Irigaray is not the first to question the equation we are used to making between clear vision and reliable knowledge. The German philosopher, Heidegger (1961: 52), criticized a desire for knowledge that took the form of requiring total visibility, since that implied the capture and surveillance of its object. At the same time, he pointed out that notions of looking were built into the foundations of Western philosophy. The clarity and abstraction that have been the hallmark of privileged knowledge begin, on this reading, to look sinister, to have their affiliations with a sort of violence and will to power.

Women have been kept from a place in the philosophical tradition. (Irigaray's own work has rarely been received or offered a reply as a contribution to the debate in philosophy; it is shunted off elsewhere, so as not to confuse the issue – see Whitford 1991: 1–3.) In the Western tradition women have been identified with the body, as distinct from the mind, with a materiality that has been opposed, traditionally, to abstraction. They have been associated with absence of knowledge, darkness, materiality. Out of this body of darkness, as it has been thought, Irigaray calls for women's voices to tell what they know. This is not a matter of spells or recipes: it is a question of hearing about ways of knowing that do not demand blinding visibility, that proceed by other techniques than threadbare logics, that feel their way by sympathy with what is outside the person wanting to know. It is not, I repeat, a matter of witchcraft, but it may involve a new attention to the religious dimension of experience, a respect for spirit, so long the disowned sister of intellect.

So we come to appreciate the brilliance of Irigaray's title: *Speculum of the Other Woman*. For it does not rest in a reference to the work of mirroring that is demanded of women, men's other, under patriarchy. It takes the name of the instrument used to make it possible to examine the hidden recesses of the female body, and so directs us to consider that unknown female darkness, the obscured desire of women. Irigaray calls it a dark centre like the pupil of the eye, *kōre* in Greek, through which we are invited to look, but inwards.

She warns us that we shall find depletion in that interior. Deprived of independent representation in culture – 'woman' is called up exclusively to perform the work of endorsing notions of 'man' and keeping them in place – living women are cut off from their origin. There are very few representations of mother–daughter relationships. Women have no sign made to them by the world that endorses their own positioning as daughters. Every woman had a mother who shared her sex and gender but in the absence of images to support that identity it is shabby and undermined by sadness.

There is no shortage, on the other hand, of images that display the relation between women and men. *Kŏre*, the Greek word Irigaray uses, can mean both the pupil of the eye and the woman, more often known as Persephone, who divided her identity between daughter and spouse. Irigaray asks for a turn into that darkness.

Not in order to find a solid treasure; this is not Aladdin's cave. Irigaray is emphatic that there will be no single answer to the question of what is the truth about women, no one form or shape to be unveiled but process itself, change, transformation, a continuous state of becoming: something like that ever-living fire, the origin from which all matter and the continuously changing universe derive, of which Heraclitus was writing a century before Plato had set down a word.

To offer to read Shakespeare's *Antony and Cleopatra* in the light of Irigaray's *Speculum* is to put her ideas to the test with a vengeance. Images of Cleopatra were made while she was alive to demonstrate her own authority: when she ruled Egypt, coins carried her head and the priests recorded her benefactions in temple inscriptions. She was shown, with her son Caesarion, in a relief the size of a hoarding, on the rear wall of the great temple at Dendera. Since that time, though, the cultures of the West have used her image for their own purposes. Since the Renaissance the figure of Cleopatra has been a linchpin in Western constructions of women and desire.

This transformation is not arbitrary or accidental. The man who made himself emperor of Rome after Antony's death, the remaining triumvir, Caesar, as he is called in the play, made his defeat of Cleopatra the symbolic basis of his own authority. He dated his rule from the day that Cleopatra died. When it was proposed to name a month in his honour, custom would have led to choosing September, when his birthday fell, but instead he settled on the month when Cleopatra died. That is how we come to call our eighth month August: for this man was to be known to history as the great Augustus. The famous *pax Augusta*, the universal peace of Augustus, claimed that it was founded on the death and defeat of Cleopatra.

All this happened two thousand years ago, at the start of the era that we are used to recognizing as our own. It was during the reign of Augustus that the founder of Christianity was born. The birth of Jesus, the sacred child, only took place in Bethlehem, away from Nazareth where his parents usually lived, because 'there went out a decree from Caesar Augustus, that all the world should be taxed' (Luke 2: 1). The Christian religion and Augustan order have been entwined from the beginning. The law, history, architecture and literature of Augustan Rome have been respected as models of civic and civilized life ever since.

So it makes sense to take images of Cleopatra seriously. What was it about her that gave her name such symbolic force? As Woolf mused: she 'must have had a way with her' (Woolf 1992: 55). There are more rewarding questions to put, though, than 'What was Cleopatra really like?'. Try asking how the *notion* of a Cleopatra offended the Romans. Under the ancient laws of Egypt, women enjoyed freedoms not permitted to women who lived under the law of Rome. Romans were particularly scandalized that Egyptian women were permitted to choose their own husbands. Daughters inherited equally with sons. In Egypt royal power could be exercised by women. Cleopatra was not just a threat to Rome's overseas territories. Her very name implied a challenge to the principle in which Roman society was grounded, the difference between men and women that was created under the law of Rome.

Roman poets and historians told her story in their terms. In a form of shorthand, Lucan, in his *Pharsalia*, called her the 'incestuous' queen (Bullough 1957–75, 5: 326). The move allowed him to repeat Rome's refusal to grant a voice in the state to women. He did not focus on her sexuality by chance: the turn towards forgetting that Cleopatra was an independent ruler of a very rich kingdom, denying how great were the means at her disposal, begins by bringing her down to the level of other women, even to the place of the least respected among them. If there is anything more alarming to the Roman than a woman with the means to get what she wants, it is the fact that she has a will of her own, her desire. They make him afraid because his culture has told him that women are not like that: could he be hallucinating?

In the Renaissance, artists and writers across Europe began to rework the figure of Cleopatra as they renewed their identification with the Roman tradition. They had to square her not only with their sense of the imperial past but also with current attempts in the cities where they lived, in Augsburg, Haarlem or Florence to lay down the terms for women's lives and for relations between the sexes. It was with one eye on the new institution of Christian marriage that they told the story of Cleopatra.

It was the same with Shakespeare, too. But let us see what happens when he sets out to tell the story of the woman outside the law. He has recently told the story of *King Lear*, the man who thought he was the law itself, and he comes with the habit of telling his stories by means of a great diversity of situated voices, not a single narrator. It is this technique that allows the material to be opened up so far, felt from so many different positions, that, like Humpty-Dumpty, it can never be put neatly together again into a simple moral. Most important of all, it means that Shakespeare will step into the place of Cleopatra, and find her voice. Centuries before Irigaray would ask for a different knowledge of women's desire, articulated by their own voices, Shakespeare was going to discover how the voice of Cleopatra destabilized the old story about women and desire, when he tried to repeat it in *Antony and Cleopatra*. When he added in the voice of Cleopatra it jammed the airwaves, fused the system.

From the opening words a possibility that the official report may be open to question is built in: after all, we are in Egypt but what we are hearing about is Rome. Shakespeare is telling a Roman story and it takes him some time to come to himself and say, wait, this story is not true. He starts off more or less in tune with the Romans, so his Act I could well be called, 'Name Cleopatra as she is called in Rome'. I shall start by working through it.

One Roman man tells another what a disgrace Antony's affair with Cleopatra is (scene i). The problem seems to centre, for the speaker, on the fact that Antony has abandoned a state of fixity and order for one of flux. It is in the poetry that this complaint is lodged; only poetry could register and examine this discomfort that makes itself known but has no recognized name. Shakespeare was a dramatic poet: his method was to use poetry as a means of exploring interaction between characters. In this play it will take him beyond the usual explanations of the familiar story he is telling. Antony's heart was satisfactory, it seems, so long as it was devoted to fighting. Then its force was channelled in a single effort, but now he has entered a state where his energy produces effects that are inconsistent and contradictory. His heart is at once a bellows blowing up flames and a fan that makes cool draughts. Antony has become an alarming presence to the Romans in proportion as he has given up being a savage one: now he is associated with homely tools and toys, instead of armour. Even the thought of the to and fro of air, suggesting the movement of breath in and out of the living body, makes the Roman speaker angry and afraid. He does not want to remember that vulnerability. He understands that the change in Antony has come about through contact with Cleopatra's sexuality and he denounces it. She is a strumpet, Antony is her kept fool.

This is evidently a world where masculinity means one thing, martial valour, and prides itself on fixity: its quality can only be contaminated by close contact with the feminine, which is defined as its degraded antithesis. It sounds uncannily close to the arrangements Irigaray described. Yet the audience may not be able to accept the speaker's account as realistic, once they have seen the principals for themselves. They may decide that they can no longer find the Roman perspective or terms much help in making sense of what is going on.

Cleopatra, when she enters, talks about setting a limit on how far she will allow herself to be loved, fusing in a single image all that might have been expected of the imperious and contrary courtesan. But she is driven by something we had not predicted, returning insistently to ask whether Antony will go back to Rome if he is sent for. Is she sparring with him, trying whom is stronger? Why the sarcastic emphasis on paying attention to what his wife and the young man in Rome want? Does Cleopatra really want him to insist on his authority as husband and older man, or is she calling him, as her boast of her own autonomy as Egypt's queen might suggest, to confront her on equal terms? Is she afraid that he is about to leave her?

How long it has taken to get to this question. To ask it, you have to be viewing Cleopatra and her feelings with respect, believing that she is like other women, and that does not come naturally in this culture. Shakespeare's first thought, like ours, is of Cleopatra's power. The result is to distance her, to obscure her vulnerability at the moment of the play's opening, when her lover may be on the point of going back to his wife. We are all caught up together in the Roman confusion: because she has wealth and power, we hear Cleopatra's voice as that of the courtesan, it does not necessarily occur to us that she may be in pain. We have agreed not to believe in her love. She is a strumpet.

It is by taking the part of Cleopatra, speaking out of the predicament he finds her to be in, that Shakespeare will find, if at all, a way that is not the Roman one to understand her story. Irigaray seemed to be calling for something rather different, the actual voice of a living woman, yet what we are offered here does go some way towards meeting her specifications. In *Antony and Cleopatra* the playwright can be heard trying out a voice for Cleopatra. He may have to start again nearly every time from one that is wilful and demanding, tuned to Roman expectations, but he will find himself striking different and unattested notes that begin to make up a song we have not heard before. We scarcely know how to listen for it. Finding this voice becomes the project of the play: that is why it will continue for a whole act after the death of Antony.

In Shakespeare's dramatization of the encounter between Antony, the Roman triumvir, and Cleopatra, the Egyptian queen, they say, you can follow in a definitive version what happens when the man of power meets the desiring woman. Let us accept those terms, for the moment, and begin to consider the impact on Antony, as it is staged here. Antony's response to Cleopatra in this opening scene, though positive, is alarming. He feels and welcomes the loss of Rome as a melting and dissolution of all fixed boundaries, including the one between animal and human worlds. As Shakespeare tells the story, it is the relationship with Cleopatra that prompts Antony's rejection of Roman order at this stage. Specifically, what he discovers of himself through his connection with her, made visible in their embrace, is so overwhelming that he has no patience for anything less. Committed Romans will read this as adolescent: it is not impossible, though, to believe that a sense of life that surpassed the Roman account might be waiting outside its confines to be discovered. Even as Antony glories in his enterprise though, he senses and gives voice to the threat it brings. He talks of the pain of punishment because he is conscious of danger in throwing down a challenge. He is putting himself in jeopardy. Rome is very powerful.

To hear the language spoken in these late poetic dramas, attend to the voices that use poetry to speak out of differing situations, and the logic that works is the logic of association, the logic of the psyche. It allows us to connect this early speech with what Antony says in Act IV, when he speaks of seeing 'a cloud that's dragonish' (IV.xv.2). Antony has come to explore the consequences for his inner consciousness of discarding those defining forms authorized by Rome. In Act IV he is experiencing himself as formless, unstable, incapable of being apprehended, and feels that the only way he can retrieve self-definition is by the Roman gesture of suicide. He cannot tolerate the fluidity. He cannot bear not being able to have a sense of a fixed identity. Defeat at Caesar's hands is only the outward manifestation of his failure to find a viable way to live outside a Roman ordering of the world. Blaming Cleopatra, attacking her, as he does repeatedly at that point, is caused by his fury at this predicament. It has been rare for critics and readers to distance themselves from these attacks. Where's the evidence? All we've seen her do is bully a messenger – so hard is it for us to believe that there is anything too bad to say about Cleopatra. Everyone knows she is not to be trusted. Who would have thought we were all such Romans at heart?

To return to the play's opening scene: Shakespeare does begin to nudge against unexpected structures of response in Cleopatra, like a swimmer who comes across what is hidden under the water by striking out through it. The Romans see only a wilful and wanton creature – the passionate gypsy – but what we hear is a shrewd and sceptical woman, not flattered by Antony's abandoned assertions, but only too aware that much of what he is saying does not add up. If the relationship with her is such a revelation to him, what was going on in his marriage? It is not a way of putting Fulvia down but a question about Roman marriage, about the relations between men and women in Rome. As an audience, readers, Romans, we are bred to be cynics, even to sneer at the simplicity of Cleopatra's question: does she not know there are other things at stake than love? Our schooling has not directed us to set much store by intimacy, and those who try to find terms in which to honour sexual feeling, like D.H. Lawrence, find language tips them over into the embarrassing forthwith. But Cleopatra's question refuses to overlook the matter of desire or leave its place in human contracts unspoken. It is through tracing her reaction to what is unliveable about the Roman way, her refusal of Roman lies, her struggle to adapt Roman formulations, that Shakespeare will locate a person that is Cleopatra. He finds her, as it were, outside Rome and works to put her into relation with it.

This will not be easy. He uses Demetrius and Philo to frame this first conversation between Antony and Cleopatra and to discover that for Romans what was at stake in it was the respect due between men –'Is Caesar with Antonius prized so slight?' (I.i.58). Cleopatra's threat is that the contract *between men* will be unsettled. To the Romans, Cleopatra and Fulvia are merely pawns in that game. It can hardly be chance that scene ii opens with a parody of this overvaluation of the male: when Shakespeare turns to imagining the forms life takes in the space outside Rome, a space that is given the name of Egypt in this play, he comes to it through the voice of a mocking woman: 'Lord Alexas, sweet Alexas, most anything Alexas, almost most absolute Alexas' (I.ii.1–2).

The authority that is refused to men at the scene's opening is gathered up and accorded here not to a person but to a form of knowledge. 'In nature's infinite book of secrecy/A little I can read' (I.ii.10–11) is all the Soothsayer will claim, but his voice sounds steadily through the chatter like a muffled drum, terse, oblique, inescapable. The special kind of fit achieved between his language and actuality will be demonstrated in the final scene. He offers a form of knowledge that is shrouded and obscure, angled like the speculum into darkness. The turn away from Rome immediately involved Shakespeare, like Irigaray, in the problem of knowing and the formulation of knowledge.

It would not be helpful or even accurate to describe the Egypt shown in Act 1, scene ii, as a world of women. Three men take part, the Roman, Enobarbas, weaves easily in and out of the conversation, and the women take it for granted that they will look to men for pleasure and for children. The talk demonstrates, though, how easily the social order based in marriage could be disrupted by the bodies of women, with their power to cuckold and to produce illegitimate children. Could this be the source of the fear that generates those fantasies of a repugnant fertility, breeding on the rampage out of control, that echo disturbingly throughout this play?

You say you have not noticed these images. Let me tune you in. Even the first and most benign of them, uttered by the Soothsayer, is more than a little unsettling. Charmian wants to know how many children she's going to have and he tells her: 'If every of your wishes had a womb,/And fertile every wish, a million' (I.ii.37–8). A teasing acknowledgement of Charmian's lively desires? Only up to a point. Under the playful surface lurks something more unpleasant, hardly palpable, the hint of a nameless spawning.

If choice of words reveals what it is that moves us, Antony's appeal to three different images of fecundity in that same Act I is one to note. Surely you have registered how he associates his anxiety about Cleopatra with a fantasy of teeming fertility:

I must from this enchanting queen break off:
Ten thousand harms, more than the ills I know,
My idleness doth hatch.

(I.ii.128–30)

Like the Soothsayer's image, it speaks of a fertility that is monstrous or encountered only in the lower forms of life and Antony admits it makes him afraid, though he cannot put a name to the threat. Perhaps we can, though: could it be that the absence of a name, the name of the father, is in itself the greatest threat? After conception, the part played by the father in procreation is invisible; it is only by giving the child his name that he can get in on the act, so to speak.

You will see for yourself how often the poetry in *Antony and Cleopatra* replays the image of engendering, of the way life begins: in mud, in courser's hairs, anywhere but in the womb, in fact. It is a restless search for alternatives, unable to settle for Agrippa's homely acceptance: 'He ploughed her, and she cropped' (II.ii.235). The play is too caught up in the very anxiety it is documenting for that. Towards the end, though, it finds its way to a clearer representation. It is the commitment to speaking out of the place of Cleopatra and, more importantly, out of her woman's body that makes it possible. At the moment when Cleopatra knows that she cannot escape the punishment the Romans have in mind for her, Shakespeare arrives at a point where the male fears that have haunted the play can be known differently. They can be presented from the point of view of the woman who is their object, their target. Cleopatra registers what the Romans would like to do to her. Refusing to go through a public humiliation in Rome, she spells out an alternative. Accepting the fact that the Romans wish to do her violence, she mirrors back in her language not only their hatred but also by means of the imagery she uses, its source:

> Rather a ditch in Egypt
> Be gentle grave unto me! Rather on Nilus' mud
> Lay me stark naked and let the water-flies
> Blow me into abhorring!

(V.ii.57–60)

It is a horrible picture, one we might be tempted and even agree to call obscene. But wait: it condenses by silent implication the fruitful swelling of the female body when it is pregnant and the morbid distension of a corpse attacked by blow-flies. The monstrous fertility attributed to other life forms earlier in the play is at last fused here with the threat of the woman's body. The fantasy speaks of hatred, a hatred directed against the maternal body, a hatred Cleopatra feels extended against herself.

Could it be that Irigaray (1991: 36–7) was not exaggerating when she made her controversial declaration that 'all of Western culture rests upon the murder of the mother'? When Shakespeare takes up his stand to speak from the place of the captured Cleopatra, the woman who has just established what the Romans have in mind for her, we seem to be hearing something very like it.

Though the Romans Philo and Demetrius may want to think of women as very different from men, the play does not endorse their efforts. Enobarbas mistakes the approach of Cleopatra for the imperious tread of his master ('Hush, here comes Anthony' (I.ii.78)). Through this figure that he developed from a mere hint in his source, Shakespeare finds an alternative voice for masculinity within the play. Perhaps because he has no position to keep up, Enobarbas does not have to pay lip-service to Roman notions. The report of Cleopatra that he gives will escape the paranoia that overtakes Antony: 'Alack, sir, no' he returns to the claim that Cleopatra is 'cunning past man's thought' (I.ii.144–5). Enobarbas has no difficulty in seeing that something is due to Cleopatra as Antony's lover, though Antony himself can find no way to admit his sense of guilt as he prepares to leave. Instead he turns on Cleopatra.

In Enobarbas Shakespeare has hit on a voice that he can set in counterpoint with the language of Roman heroism and so unsettle the audience in its acceptance of that way of thinking and talking. Enobarbas makes it impossible to overlook the gap between Antony's grand talk of state business and the shabby truth that he is deserting Cleopatra. At this stage we probably still identify with Antony enough to enjoy hearing Enobarbas being told to be quiet. It will be some time before we are brought to listen anxiously for the guidance he can offer. The audience will take refuge in the judgement of Enobarbas in the confusion after Actium (Act III, scene xiii). Who went wrong? 'Anthony only', Enobarbas replies, when Cleopatra asks if she, too, was responsible for the defeat (III.xiii.3).

At the start of the play, Enobarbas is sceptical, like the audience, about Cleopatra's performance as the great lover, but this stops well short of radical mistrust. It is with his level voice that Shakespeare will choose to carry the word of Cleopatra's splendour into the heart of the Roman camp. We realize that it is the first account of her that has not been sneering, bitter or contemptuous. The barge speech of Enobarbas in Act II, scene ii, will move into a new register altogether. It is a reaching out, an extension of language towards an experience that no attempt is made to contain. Although it describes, it is not primarily concerned to capture an image by gazing but is built up by appeals to the other senses, above all to touch and the sense of rhythm. It offers a new way of approaching Cleopatra, of respecting her mystery. What Enobarbas communicates in his famous account of Cleopatra's arrival at Cydnus is wonder, something close to a religious experience. That is how he comes to a close by associating her with 'the holy priests' (II.ii.246).

The work of discovering a voice for Cleopatra and uncovering the relation she feels with the order in which she must live is carried on by inhabiting her position in dialogue with Antony. Her performance of the part of great lover that Enobarbas was so justly sceptical about gives way, in Act I, scene iii, to sheer exasperation, when Antony tries to keep her at arm's length and leave without unpleasantness. In this reasonable anger, she asks what has changed between them that Antony should leave. Nothing: this prompts a challenge that finds its target. Is he the greatest soldier or the greatest liar in the world? The audience does not know yet that this may be the central question that the play raises; can these soldiers do anything but lie? Antony can return no satisfactory reply to her probing and it looks as if he will just leave, enraged. It is now that we see Cleopatra reach out, through the unyielding forms available to her, for the contact she is seeking. ''Tis sweating labour' (I.iii.94), she says, breaking all decorum, but she finds a way to bend the Roman language of dignity to her purpose, call him back and make sure that though she must let him go, no rupture has taken place.

Rome itself, embodied in the person of Caesar, feels that Cleopatra has it in her power to undo the whole social order. Distinction of gender is being undone, he complains (I.iv.5–7). This fear is as prominent in his account as the way Antony is failing his partners; the social enterprise will give way if this goes on. Other distinctions are at risk, too; incest is hinted at and the collapse of hierarchy. As Caesar recoils from the thought of knaves that smell of sweat we remember Cleopatra's recent talk of her own 'sweating labour'. Maybe Caesar is right. This is not paranoia; it is true that in some way Cleopatra is really antithetical to this way of ordering the world. This is the moment, though, when we are going to hear what the Romans valued in Antony, what it meant to be a good soldier, when he was still doing his duty. Caesar's reminiscence is drawn directly from North, the values have a long pedigree.[5] The mark of the best soldiers, it seems, is to suppress human instincts of revulsion and become animals. Antony browsed the bark of trees once and drank horse piss. He seemed to thrive on it. It is going to be hard to make the Roman vocabulary of 'devotion', 'office', 'honour' square with those tastes. Though the language will expose its own absurdities, as in Shakespeare's hands language is so often made to, and in the process show Rome as woefully self-deceived, the miracle is that Antony's value will be preserved. He will be felt as a hero at the end of the play, in spite of the botched suicide, because Enobarbas, Cleopatra and even Caesar have not been able to stop loving him.

For one last time before Act I closes the play returns to the puzzle of Cleopatra. She is found on a couch, calling for opiates, exactly as the propaganda would have her, in Act I, scene v. (Shakespeare never shows, any more than Cecil B. DeMille did, that Cleopatra had any administrative duties as ruler.) We know why Caesar values Antony; can Cleopatra be made to put into words what Antony means to her? The predictable wilfulness of the opening is left behind, the interaction begins to resonate when Cleopatra turns to Mardian. She addresses him chillingly, as if he were not human: 'Hast thou affections?' (I.v.12). He answers with complete linguistic poise, 'Not in deed, madam, for I can do nothing' (I.v.15). When he admits that he can be sexually roused by fantasy, she turns away. A fin has broken the surface; what is a man? is Mardian one?, what part does language play in making a man? the play asks. Cleopatra offers her own answer. She begins in the memory of sexual pleasure, groaning 'O happy horse, to bear the weight of Anthony!' (I.v.21). Without a pause, though, she moves on to ask who is Antony – the public man, the demi-Atlas, sharing Rome with Caesar, or the murmuring voice on the pillow. At the memory of this vulnerable intimacy, her mood changes. To tell this story Shakespeare had to stand where he could amplify the voice of a woman moved by desire: he discovers the shift of mood, the retreat. She wasn't born yesterday, can she still be loved? Better to think of when she was young and could be sure that she was still delectable. She speaks of herself, as the men in the play will do, as a titbit; she can point to her success in the past with famous men. But the poetry has taken Cleopatra and the play with her into a new place where tenderness and human identity are to be discovered by means of the pleasures of the body. This is one of the first attempts to find terms that do not already exist for articulating the central relationship of the play.

The scene ends on a more disturbing note. The impulse to maintain some form of intimacy with Antony, even at a distance, dominates Cleopatra. It is not clear whether it is disturbing her judgement or that there has never been any check to her will. She screws a reading of his mood out of a report, then boasts of the resources she is prepared to squander, including human lives, in order to keep in touch with him. We see her offer Charmian violence when challenged. Though the scene may have started in emotional cliché – a male dream of how a queen who was missing him might behave – it has found its way to authenticity, a place of emotional truth. It dramatizes the sense of danger that the thought of intimacy brings at the start of this play. Perhaps intimacy between women is the most frightening of all.

I move now to Act II and beyond that to reflecting on the three deaths. With the opening of the second act, the terms on which men manage to keep relations between themselves going, the public contract, begin to be examined. You could call it 'the word of war'; Caesar accuses Antony, 'You were the word of war' (II.ii.48) and in this act the words the Romans use constantly demand our attention. (By Act III, Antony's name will be more ambiguously 'the magical word of war' (II.i.31) and by Act IV he is 'poor Anthony! . . .') (IV.i.16). The story to be told is one of violence and treachery but the language of Roman honour is not designed to follow these contours closely. Men walk on stage talking; it takes a while to realize that Pompey, though he is talking about the gods and justice, is in fact referring to going to war. His relevance to the main plot seems slight until you realize that through his story Shakespeare is able to throw the rules of the Roman game into question. Other men do not seem to find it odd that Pompey should solemnly practise the forms of Rome and appeal to its values while breaking its law.

The point is, he is a man and other men can do business with him. They talk the same language; does this begin to sound like the hommosocial economy described by Irigaray? Oddly enough, a salient term in this discourse is woman. Pompey deals with his anxiety about the triumvirs by turning to the figure of Cleopatra; he bolsters his own confidence by speaking slightingly of her, making little of her power as 'Egypt's widow' (II.i.37). The triumvirs themselves take it further; they turn to the figurative use of women to pave the way to peace between them. After 40 lines of bickering, Caesar and Antony come together in agreeing that Antony's dead wife, Fulvia, was impossible, because she would not be governed. When the crisis between them peaks over the rude things Antony was unwise enough to say when Caesar's letters came, honour, the sacred honour, is restored by an apology which shifts the blame on to Fulvia and Cleopatra together.

The forms of Rome, its decorum, are what is sacred and they are secured by assigning all that has to be deplored as indecorous to the figures of absent women. ''Tis noble spoken', Lepidus applauds (II.ii.103), so we do not miss the connection; language maintains the fictions, the lies, shall we call them, of Rome. There is one more thing to be done, though. How is the accord between Antony and Caesar to be secured? Agrippa has a plan. Octavia, Caesar's sister, could be married to Antony and that would see to it. It seems that Octavia has beauty and general graces that 'speak/That which none else can utter' (II.ii.136–7). It is the men's fantasy that her person has the ability to settle meaning and that this settlement will produce peace. Given in marriage, Octavia will dispel jealousy and fear. She will guarantee the contract between men. The play's most powerful comment on the transaction may well lie in the speed with which it is left behind. Frankly if indelicately described as 'The business we have talked of' (II.ii.173), it must be got out of the way before they go off to tackle Pompey. (It is in the name of another absent woman, Antony's mother, that peace will be made with him (II.vi.46–8)). The docile Octavia now staged is nothing but their puppet: is this what marriage has to mean in Rome?

No wonder that once Antony has found a woman not schooled for this part, Cleopatra, he will never consent to give her up. Romans see it as his greatest folly – some critics, too – but this is not compulsory. There is no need to talk of transcendent love, either, to explain why there is something to be valued in their relationship. This is what the play slowly discovers.

There is no question, from early on, but that Antony is doomed. The Soothsayer frames it for him at II.iii.16–28; he cannot thrive in the context of Caesar. We might say that the man of dimmer responsiveness is better suited for life in Rome. Antony is disabled. He cannot be realistic. To say with complacence that he 'make[s] this marriage for [his] peace' but his pleasure lies elsewhere (II.iii.37–8) is only possible because Romans are trained to overlook the gap between word and actuality. The pleasure Antony speaks of must destroy both the marriage and the peace. Caesar would not be liable to this folly, since he would be indifferent to the pleasure lying beyond the Roman scheme. But pleasure is a word that may be used in our culture pejoratively; let us slide sideways to terms like 'play' and 'tenderness', terms associated with innocence if not with masculinity. Caesar is indifferent to them – see him with his sister – but it is Antony's gift for them all that makes him so loved.

It is Antony's failures of realism in Acts III and IV that drive Enobarbas and Cleopatra to desperation. It breaks the heart of Enobarbas, literally, to do it but in the end he cannot stomach Antony's ungrounded bravado and has to leave him. There is no escape for Enobarbas, though, as a second Roman who knows how to love. By giving his death such prominence the play obliges us to register that an entirely rational action might also be described as an act of treachery and that disintegration might be the price of underestimating the energy of love. This is not a Roman understanding, but towards the end the play moves out towards a place beyond; it rests in the space it has called Egypt.

That is the place where Antony kills himself. Cleopatra has not made the mistake of Enobarbas, she is still with Antony, though struggling ever more frantically with his delusional attacks on her. As the play moves towards freeing itself of them, they become more firmly attributed to Antony, though an audience may not be able to give them up on their own account. Critics do not always. The play has abandoned its repetitious staging of the imperious wanton. This may have been easier once Cleopatra's defeat at Actium had come into range; once she is humbled, tenderness is admitted to the stage. 'Fall not a tear', says Antony, and who will censure him? It is no longer a matter of boasting if he claims 'one of them rates/All that is won and lost' (III.xi.68–9). Winning and losing kingdoms, he perceives now, are no way to measure life. The audience may be baffled by the emotion it suffers at this point. It is because the play can imagine beyond Antony to Cleopatra that his failure and the failure of Rome in him can be contemplated without panic.

Being brave and generous, keeping one's word, have been called the marks of a man. It is the word that is the problem, though, here. The courage of Antony never fails, even though the audience is increasingly aware, with Cleopatra, of how weak his judgement is. His foolish personal challenge to Caesar in Act IV brings such embarrassment because it makes it impossible to keep on respecting him. We want to honour him, but it is too risky: he is making a fool of himself. Cleopatra shows us how it can be done, so that it is the form in which his courage has been cast, the Roman rituals of manhood, that his clumsy and undignified death brings into ridicule, rather than himself. What the play does not do is gloss over the unreliability of his word. He is not meaning to lie, as the life ebbs from him, but the language at his disposal leads him into falsehood. 'Of Caesar seek your honour with your safety' (IV.xvi.48): in order to utter this heroic advice, Antony has to suppress what he really knows all the time, that of course the Romans will want to humiliate Cleopatra. (We have seen him heap abuse on her himself, but the connection between Antony's hostility and the cruelty she will inspire in others is left for us to explore.) Proculeius, the man he advises her to trust, is the one who will betray her to Caesar. It is a matter of almost unbearable poignancy for the audience to be forced to recognize how unreliable and how confused he is in his attempt to protect Cleopatra. The language he speaks comes between him and understanding.

Roman legions used to be led by a standard crowned with a brazen wreath. You may have seen pictures of them. They are symbols of the martial power of Rome, part of the language by which it defined itself. There have been many occasions throughout the action where Cleopatra has been seen struggling, sometimes awkwardly, to adapt the language of Rome to describe or analyse her own experience. 'These hands do lack nobility that they strike/A meaner than myself' (II.v.83–4). The fit has been uneasy, but she has no independent vocabulary of her own to use. At the end of the play the tacit critique performed by her borrowings becomes much harder to ignore, as our sympathy is permitted to linger with her in defeat. At the moment of Antony's death she famously exclaims 'O, withered is the garland of the war,/The soldiers' pole is fall'n' (IV.xvi.66–7). Behind these words lies the discarded image of the brazen standard carried in front of the legions.

The pretence that change and decay could be resisted, the fantasy of heroic indifference and impermeability in which Rome gloried, is here set aside. Antony's silenced body lies on the stage. To do that fact justice, Cleopatra's language has to rework Rome's and in the process to expose the lies it tells.

Cleopatra begins to become a reliable figure for the audience when she mourns for Antony. If we believed in him at all, it is possible now to consider trusting what Cleopatra says. Her threat lifted, at least temporarily, she can put it to us that all the fantasies were misplaced, all we see in her is a woman. The passion that Rome deemed terrifying or scandalous actually made her vulnerable, brought her to this loss. She will have no more mythology: where the Romans talked of Mars, it is farmgirls and housewives, women who work for their bread, who are the figures with whom Cleopatra asks to be compared. Her desire is no different from theirs. That is what has been regularly despised and traduced in the play, in the name of order.

Feeling Cleopatra now as a heroine, however precariously – how can she find something brave and noble to do, when those words always defined male behaviour – the play moves into the challenge of rewriting the Roman order. 'Written in our flesh' might be a title for Act V. If the truth is now going to be told, it is the truth about the cruelty and treachery of Rome. A man comes on carrying a trophy, the sword he has pulled reeking out of Antony's body. The words spoken over it can deceive no longer: they are excuses, bids to appease guilt, at best, the admission of pain. Cleopatra's case, however, is going to prove the status of Roman claims to integrity once and for all.

At this moment of triumph, it is Caesar's overriding concern to justify himself, to contain his actions within the linguistic register of Rome. Although betrayal and violence are endemic in Rome – Pompey would have liked his inferiors to take responsibility for cutting the cable on his galley so he could take the triumvirs captive – there are no terms in use to acknowledge this. 'Honourable' and 'kindly' are the words Caesar chooses to characterize his intentions towards Cleopatra; she is not the only one he wants to tell that Caesar 'cannot live/To be ungentle' (V.i.59–60). While he is waiting to hear from her, he takes his friends off to examine the writings that will prove that though he may have been carrying on a war, really he was 'calm and gentle' (V.i.75).

Against these now patent lies stand the facts of Cleopatra's predicament. Proculeius, Caesar's envoy, distracts her with a pretence of conversation in order to trap and overpower her. Cleopatra does not kill herself until she has confirmed her suspicion that in spite of his repeated protestations, Caesar means to display her as his trophy through the streets of Rome. The Romans would do anything to dissemble the cruelty that she accurately divines in this.

Antony and Cleopatra is a very confusing play. It undermines and goes beyond the order that readers and audiences are used to operating by: what is a man? what is a woman? what are they calling love? it asks. How can we answer, when it is our own language, the language of Rome, that this very play has exposed as lies? It is easier to settle, as critics very often do, for arguing about exactly how far Cleopatra was at fault or how much she really loved Mark Antony. Can the play qualify as an example of 'transcendent love', they judiciously enquire. Quietly, the very machinery the play has been dismantling is reinstalled, the questions it raised are suppressed, the notions it discredited are rehabilitated. Let us refuse to make that move. There is every reason to decline it. By the end of the play it is not her relation with Antony that is our focus; Cleopatra herself has moved to the centre of the stage.

The play has escaped from the old project of representing woman in order to define man. Finding a voice for Cleopatra has obliged Shakespeare to discover that there is an unknown and unsuspected sub-jectivity at the site previously veiled in fantasies. Through the poetry he begins to explore that subjectivity as it exists after Antony's removal. It is a little like stepping off the edge of the world, doing the impossible, offering to refute Irigaray's charge. Unexpectedly, however, it confirms her most radical assertions.

Cleopatra is not confined by her relation to Antony after he is dead; her grief makes up only a part of her experience. She is defined much more emphatically by her relation to other women. It is to these she turns in the moment of self-knowledge after loss. Rejecting titles like 'empress' or 'royal Egypt' she reaches out, even to the poorest labouring women, knowing that their longings are no different from hers:

No more but e'en a woman, and commanded
By such poor passion as the maid that milks
And does the meanest chores.

(IV.xvi.74–6)

It is hard to give this moment weight enough: we are so well schooled in overlooking or depreciating the connections between women, so quick to reward the ones who will settle for a separate peace. It is not just a verbal point, either. Shakespeare puts Charmian and Iras to stand beside Cleopatra and talk with her through the final scenes where she is betrayed by Proculeius, Seleucus and Caesar, one after another, till the women escape together from the abuse and treachery of Rome. Without Irigaray's voice we might have no means of framing that final movement of the play, no feeling for its Utopian speculation. Free at last from the repetition of fantasies, the play reaches obscurely after a knowledge of ordinary women that is still not articulated in Rome today. It acknowledges the connections between women, the play of sympathy and intelligence that takes place among them, and it suggests that what these connections underpin is the women's sense of identity. One of Cleopatra's most anguished replies to Antony's attack was 'Not know me yet?' (III.xiii.158). Perhaps this was what she was asking for all along: to see herself, however darkly, in the speculum of the other woman.

The unconscious exists, they say, outside time. It knows no history, only a continuous present.[6] Such was not the case, though, with the writing of this play, which took place in a certain town, London, at a certain moment around 1608, to put it deliberately loosely. By looking through the speculum of Irigaray, I have given up any attempt to read historically, to set the play in the context of debate and political change in which meanings are forged. I have written as if the play were made and watched in Italy or France, making no allowance for the differences of religion and nationality that would have limited and shaped its reception. This ahistorical reading cannot be adequate, alone. It must be relevant, for instance, that England was already trying to develop an overseas empire of its own, like Rome's. I do not believe, though, that the reading based on Irigaray that I have offered would easily be invalidated by any historical information. The real limitation of this theoretical position lies in its failure to offer tools for addressing the part played in Western culture by the representation of race. A whole dimension is missing if we overlook how Cleopatra's race functions in the play. Shakespeare's imagination may be able to reconcile her with less privileged women, but it preserves a chasm between her dark self and the white women of Rome. Without tools for reading this persistence, there can be no carrying through Irigaray's project of understanding the ways that we use sexual difference to structure our account of the world and to hide the truth about women's lives.

SUPPLEMENT

NIGEL WOOD: You make the point on p. 76 that Shakespeare's *poetry* helps the play emerge from 'Roman' mastery. Is the route to such emancipation a poetic one? What would be the full consequences (critical and social) of the fulfilment of Irigaray's call that an independent female voice be fully heard – not as some constructed Other, but rather in terms of 'difference'?

MARY HAMER: Do you mean to ask if I think poetry the *only* route out of the particular cast of patriarchal thought we have inherited in the West? I wouldn't say that, no. Poetry offers certain chances. Other people besides Shakespeare can find fresh ways to name and examine their experience by using poetry. That is, by agreeing to accept the games that language plays, the images it billows into, the rhymes and puns you didn't necessarily intend, to accept the music language makes with itself as an important part of the way that we may make sense with words. New sense can be made like this, and the mastery of Roman vision and language be challenged. Another way is through drama, drama rather than debate: when you have heard voices speak out of differing situations, locations of feeling, which is what drama is made out of, you've learned to pay attention to competing realities. It makes it harder to accept simple answers, the ones that involve the silencing of voices.

The full consequences of women speaking: what would happen if the rainbow broke into flower? Setting aside that dangerous comparison between women and the natural world, one which has always meant trouble for us, let's pursue my real intention, which was to indicate that we were moving into a dimension that's still not explored. Would you settle for some initial observations? It is still hard to speak with authority as a woman unless you speak the language of men, the language of Rome. Attempts to unsettle this language get women in trouble: look what happened to Irigaray. But using this language is bad for them, mis-represents them to themselves. It is in conversations between those women who can agree to try to make safe spaces to work together that change has a chance to begin. It's not at all easy finding out what you have to say and learning to recognize and respect your own voice: there is a high degree of emotional and physical stress, fear, in short, for many women in unlearning these old lessons.

And when enough of us have – for one independent female voice won't go very far, will it? – what might be the result? Most of us live in some sort of relationship with men, family members and colleagues as well as lovers, and this living connection means that they will perhaps have begun changing with us: they may be more able to hear what we have to say, less dominated by their own fantasies of what we 'must' mean, both literally and emotionally. We will not all be saying the same thing, we women; don't expect a programme for the future to emerge. But in our impatience of the forms of knowledge that were founded on a fantasy of who we were, we will be asking for realism, for a common language that will let us all address the uncertainty of our shared human life, and our shared responsibility for everything that lives. If *Antony and Cleopatra* is to be trusted, it is the refusal to value what is living, vulnerable and in process that poisons the world of Rome.

NW: I'd appreciate your extending your range a little here to take in a consideration of the place of historical information in critical analysis. You conclude on p. 88 by affirming that, although one could explore the specific historical location of texts, such an approach would not necessarily alter the basic psychic patterns you describe. Why not?

MH: It's a question of underlying structures, rather than supporting detail. Let me explain. In spite of the fact that meanings are unstable and constantly renegotiated from one time and place to another, familiar patterns, as Barrett says ('The place of aesthetics in Marxist criticism', in Nelson and Grossberg 1988: 697–713) keep popping up. In my book *Signs of Cleopatra* (1993), I set out to make specifically historical readings of representations of Cleopatra produced at different times and places in Europe since the Renaissance. I repeatedly confirmed that to understand these images, to read them in their detail and specificity, you had to be able to reinsert them in the debates – about marriage or the franchise or Newtonian optics – in which they were produced. Information about the actual historical Cleopatra, the Ptolemaic queen, was no help. In this sense, every Cleopatra was different and required historical explication to become legible. Great fun it was, too, working each of them out.

On the other hand, and this is why I'm so confident in saying I don't think the basic psychic patterns would be altered, my research showed that the figure of Cleopatra was being used, consistently, as the means of working out what men thought. It's no exaggeration to say that thought, cultural development, was taking place through the act of representing Cleopatra: which is exactly what Irigaray would lead us to expect. The male writers and painters I studied were not interested in her as a person. It was her name that challenged them because it signalled desire and authority at once, lodged together in a woman's body. The name of Cleopatra is probably the best shorthand we have in the West for active desire in a woman. In all the cases I studied, that desire was not investigated or invited to speak for itself but treated as an object of danger, scepticism or contempt. Does this begin to remind you of the Romans? Irigaray would say treating women's desire like this was a fundamental characteristic of the culture we have derived through Rome.

NW: Can Irigaray's perceptions be applied equally valuably to other texts, Shakespearian or not? Which?

MH: I'd certainly have thought so. *Antony and Cleopatra* was an ideal text to try her theories out on because it faces the question of women, desire, and culture head on, as it were. But Irigaray is making a point about the way the figure of 'woman' is used in *all* Western writing. So texts where women play a less prominent part than in *Antony and Cleopatra* and even texts where women are not represented directly at all can still be investigated using her ideas. It is the part played by a fiction of the feminine in constructing the West's leading fiction of stable masculinity that she urges us to recognize and question.

Having said that, I do believe that there are plays of Shakespeare that would be especially interesting to think through in that way. What would happen, for instance, if you brought *The Winter's Tale* or *King Lear* into alignment with Irigaray's ideas? They might be surprisingly congenial partners, you know. Do you remember that crowning moment of *The Winter's Tale* when Hermione comes to life and starts to speak? It is not to her husband but to her daughter that she turns. Shakespeare highlights the very relationship, the one between mother and daughter, that Irigaray notes as usually missing from representation. What process of the imagination can have led him to that place, after starting the play with such a strong attack on women? I imagine Irigaray's thought could help us make sense of it.

We're not writing poetic dramas, it's true, but we might be able to lever ourselves into a fresh position, too, using the purchase Irigaray offers. It does mean a huge shift, though. What would happen, I ask myself, if we started thinking about Lear as a man who tries to control what his daughters say about him, censor what they are allowed to make known as the truth about their relationship with their father?

CHAPTER 4

Antony and Cleopatra
and Genre Criticism

ROBERT WILCHER

[Robert Wilcher's study of generic approaches to literature has in view the critical mystification where *Antony and Cleopatra* is concerned. In order that we may avoid undue critical preconception, and forsake even the most deep-seated recognitions as to what is truly a 'tragic' emotion (usually Aristotelian in inspiration), we must account for deviation as well as development. If we depart from a more or less stable set of aesthetic frames for critical judgement, then we may be prey to the anarchy of non-meaning which comes to be underpinned by a critic's self-projection. Yet even this reflection does not do justice to the project to discover a basic calculus of readerly or audience response. What it does *not* attempt to do is simply read off new or experimental works against some transhistorical template.

To identify norms of expectation (either authorial or readerly) is not at the same time to ground such types of comprehension outside of history. For Jonathan Culler, in his *Structuralist Poetics* (1975), any culture develops a 'competence' at understanding literary expression, a 'set of conventions for reading texts' (Culler 1975: 118) that spells literature. Although not ever capable of absolute certainty, and at times knowing that it is a critical short-cut, we rely on an 'author' as an authoritative critical item. We try to identify the 'significant attitude' of the author or at least a common denominator for a work's overall metaphorical coherence, a comfortable 'fit' between some implied intention and cultural expectation (Culler 1975: 115). This may seem to elide a crucial distinction, between an author about whom we may be able to garner verifiable information (true of one instance of writing) and our historically relative frames which determine where we look to discover facts about the author (which add up because there are always certain criteria of relevance operative now that could not have been then). If we weight the latter alternative, then such scepticism at historical information merely replaces one monolithic concept (the biographical/historical author) with another (the faith that we can grasp the totality of now and sum it up regardless of distinctions of class, race or gender in a blanket assertion of relevance; see also Culler 1981: 51–4).

Looking at this a little more positively, we could also conclude that this perception actually allows us to study these cultural forms of comprehension as they succeed each other throughout history. For Ferdinand de Saussure, in his *Course in General Linguistics* (1915), the bias towards historical descriptions based on notions of development ('diachronic' explanations) always militates against wider accounts of causation and influence that derive from a fuller consideration of contemporaneous factors ('synchronic' explanations). At any time discourse (not restricted to the verbal as narrowly defined, but indicating all forms of expression) operates according to the tacit rules that actually constitute it as a comprehensible act. While most speech acts are individual in themselves (described as *parole* by Saussure), they are only comprehensible because they are a choice within an abstract grammar (*langue*). Of necessity, *langue* can never appear in any one instance, yet in an enlarged sense it is present in every utterance from that discourse. Identify the discourse and you would be capable of producing a series of utterances all apparently individual, yet the guarantee of such particularity is the abstract network of rules that renders it comprehensible.

For Wilcher, genres behave as a *langue* for all attempts to identify form in drama. It is essential to stress that they are never formulaic or predictive. On the contrary, they are inevitably involved in any audience response, and gesture to many assumptions that generate any sense of shared culture. For the linguist, Noam Chomsky, this interaction between theory and practice was actually a dialectic between 'competence' (largely in Culler's sense) and 'performance', the path towards the recognition of a grammatically well-formed and so expressive sentence. But what if literary or more specifically dramatic expressiveness stems from a hybridity of formal indications, where there is a danger (or opportunity) for the exception to disprove the rule? Were those who attended performances of Shakespeare's work a unitary audience?

A generic study has to step outside the historically contingent ('What we can now identify as a likely Jacobean audience . . .') to embrace a type of understanding that still changes but particularly slowly. For Alastair Fowler, in his *Kinds of Literature* (1982), literary understanding is of works, not of aggregates of words, of rhetorical orders, not of local effects. From this perspective, the 'diachronic' is a far more useful grid for analysis than the 'synchronic', as the historical (successive states of being or development) cannot ever be securely hived off from the present. To identify the author of a *parole* is not to reduce such a being to a bare function (see Fowler 1982: 49–53). The obligation to provide 'constructive inference' (Fowler 1982: 52) when understanding even the most basic information derives from a conception of audience response that is constituted by the previous plays we have seen, even if we have never ever read Aristotle's *Poetics* to tell us how the best dramatists have written tragedies. Fowler's work is dedicated to E.D. Hirsch, Jr, the author of widely influential studies of literary meaning, the most famous of which are his *Validity in Interpretation* (1967) and *Aims of Interpretation* (1976). For Hirsch, the central task of critical work is to strive towards *objective* knowledge, an always communal activity. Just as an author's original meaning can imply numerous later formulations of its 'type idea', it is possible to deduce the shape or 'intrinsic genre' of the work one is engaged in reading: 'the type that determines the boundaries of an utterance as a whole' (Hirsch 1967: 89). As we read, preliminary guesses as to what kind of writing we are deciphering give place to a more and more consistent grasp of its particular meaning – but the route there has always been guided by our prior mastery of norms and rules.

For Hirsch, interpretation of a work is quite a different task from that of assessing its significance. 'Meaning' implies an aim of the recovery of original intention, whereas 'significance' names the evaluative relationship between that work and 'a person, or a conception, or a situation, or indeed anything else imaginable' (Hirsch 1967: 8). You can demonstrate error or validity in the ascertaining of 'meaning', yet hardly do the same with the description of a relationship. In terms that resemble Culler's 'competence', Hirsch lays great store by probability judgements (or informed guesses): a 'rational means of reaching conclusions in the absence of directly experienced certitude' (Hirsch 1967: 175), yet Culler's treatment of this pretextual store of literary knowledge is also a means of answering such questions as 'Whose rationality?' and 'What is its agenda?'. Are experienced readers always the 'best' readers of literature?

For Northrop Frye, this process of putting one's experience as a reader to work is far less a case of objective mastery. Commencing with several studies on Romanticism, and Blake in particular, he identified several guiding myths or narratives that rewrote Scripture as a secular document, imbued with imaginative power. Narrative was not just some linear path, but a syndrome or pattern that aspired to the symbolic and thus to the perception of several alternative, yet simultaneous, levels of meaning. His *Anatomy of Criticism* (1957) undertook to look at structures of understanding that were far deeper than a well-honed literary education could provide. These were archetypal in scope, and appeared across a wide range of writing by a variety of (at first) widely disparate authors. *Anatomy of Criticism* was divided into four sections, on 'Modes', 'Symbols', 'Myths' and 'Genres', and its main aim was to suggest a 'genuine poetics' that constructed 'a systematic structure of knowledge' (Frye 1957: 18). Without this (and we may read this with Fowler in mind), literature is not a 'piled aggregate of "works"', but rather an 'order of words', shaped and developed not anarchically, but rather with the attainment of *shared* pattern in mind. This puts in severe doubt the 'absurd quantum formula of criticism' that takes as its goal the

' "getting out" of a poem exactly what the poet may vaguely be assumed to have been aware of "putting in" '. This 'slovenly illiteracy' turns out to be naïvely inductive, no matter how rigorous in its values it may appear to be (Frye 1957: 16–17). 'Genre' in Frye's poetics approximates to the more social world of event and process, the more or less conscious invocation of specifically literary forms, that promotes parody and allusion (see Frye 1957: 243–51). This deployment, and rhetorical manipulation, of known forms is not divorced from deeper psychic or spiritual structures, yet its method of hailing its audience is subtly different. This kind of address to the reader/viewer may seem to deliver a purely literary response, yet Frye (and Wilcher) have this emphasis suggest wider connections – with the present as well as the Jacobean past.

NIGEL WOOD

I

In the long history of critical debate about *Antony and Cleopatra*, questions of interpretation and judgement have frequently turned on the issue of the play's genre. Early in the nineteenth century, Samuel Taylor Coleridge (1907: 97) was tempted to consider it 'a formidable rival' of *Macbeth*, *King Lear*, *Hamlet* and *Othello*; whereas at the beginning of the twentieth, Bradley (1909: 282) argued that such an 'error in valuation' could only arise because of 'a failure to discriminate the peculiar marks of *Antony and Cleopatra* itself, marks which, whether or not it be the equal of the earlier tragedies, make it decidedly different'. Having attempted to account for this difference, Bradley (1909: 305) concluded that the play was, nevertheless, 'a great tragedy'. Later commentators have been more discriminating as to its generic status. Stauffer's (1949: 247) verdict is that it 'is not the next-to-the-last of the tragedies, but the first and greatest of the dramatic romance'; Schanzer (1963: 183) makes a case for its being 'the most quintessential of Shakespeare's Problem Plays'; and Brodwin (1972: 223), distinguishing it from tragedies of Courtly Love like *Romeo and Juliet*, describes it as 'the greatest tragedy of Worldly Love ever to have been written'.

It is not surprising that the critical history of *Antony and Cleopatra* is strewn with such endeavours to place it in relation to other works of a similar kind or in relation to some more general notion of tragedy or romance, because – as Fowler (1982: 259) puts it in the most comprehensive formulation of contemporary genre theory – the 'processes of generic recognition are in fact fundamental to the reading process'. Fowler's emphasis on a reader's need to be alert to the generic features of a text and his acknowledgement that reading itself is a *process* both derive from a significant reorientation in thinking about the status and function of genre study as a critical tool. In the wake of the Romantic reaction against the predominantly rule-bound and prescriptive bias of neoclassical criticism, Benedetto Croce (1866–1952) had argued that the attempt to categorize works of literature was contrary to the very nature of the creative impulse and could only inhibit or distort the responses of reader or audience (Croce 1968). Over the past few decades, however, the value – indeed, the necessity – of 'generic recognition' as an enabling factor in the production of both texts and readings has been asserted across a wide spectrum of theoretical practices.

Approaching the act of reading from the perspective of hermeneutics, for example, Hirsch (1967: 72–3) highlights the primary importance of genre:

> quite aside from the speaker's choice of words, and, even more remarkably, quite aside from the context in which the utterance occurs, the details of meaning that an interpreter understands are powerfully determined and constituted by his meaning expectations. And these expectations arise from the interpreter's conception of the type of meaning that is being expressed. . . . Furthermore, these expectations could have arisen only from a genre idea: 'In this type of utterance, we expect these types of traits.'

From the different perspective of reception theory, Hans Robert Jauss is concerned with the active part played by the reader in realizing the aesthetic effects of a literary text, which he sees as underlying and prior to interpretation. He draws attention to the centrality of genre for an analysis of 'the response and the impact of a work within the definable frame of reference of the reader's experience' (Jauss 1970: 11). In his account of the ideas of Tzvetan Todorov, Scholes (1974: 128) indicates the contribution that structuralism has made to the development of a modern theory of genre:

> Every literary text is a product of a preexisting set of possibilities, and it is also a transformation of those possibilities. Therefore, literary study must operate by proceeding from the set of possibilities toward the individual work, or from the work toward the set of possibilities – which is, in fact, a generic concept. Genres are the connecting links between individual literary works and the universe of literature.

Jonathan Culler explores the significance of these connecting links in relation to the concept of 'literary competence' which makes possible the act of reading an individual work *as literature*:

> Since literature is a second-order semiotic system which has language as its basis, a knowledge of language will take one a certain distance in one's encounter with literary texts, and it may be difficult to specify precisely where understanding comes to depend on one's supplementary knowledge of literature. But the difficulty of drawing a line does not obscure the palpable difference between understanding the language of a poem, in the sense that one could provide a rough translation into another language, and understanding the poem.
>
> (Culler 1975: 114)

This 'supplementary knowledge' consists of a familiarity with various conventions, which are 'the constituents of the institution of literature' and which govern the process of writing as well as the process of reading. In order to produce a literary text, a writer must 'engage with a literary tradition'; and this activity

> is made possible by the existence of the genre, which the author can write against, certainly, whose conventions he may attempt to subvert, but which is none the less the context within which his activity takes place, as surely as the failure to keep a promise is made possible by the institution of promising.
>
> (Culler 1975: 116)

Fundamental to Culler's theory of literary competence is the argument that it 'depends on mastery of a system', which can be taught and which must be internalized in the same way that grammar has to be internalized in order to acquire competence in a language. Scholes also directs attention to the pedagogical implications of foregrounding the role of genre in the transactions among writer, text and reader. He identifies the teacher's task as that of helping students 'to learn the grammar of literary forms by showing them aspects of this grammar as an abstract way of organizing individual texts – but a way which has historical validity as well as conceptual convenience' (Culler 1975: 114; Scholes 1974: 129). Fowler is equally careful to stress the need for a historical dimension in setting out a sequence of steps for the reception of a text by a critical reader. The first phase, 'construction – that is, determining the features of the work intended', is a matter of asking what signals were originally sent, what local meanings were originally conveyed, what conventions were used, what innovations or variations were effected within the current 'generic horizon':

> Genre can be a powerful instrument in construction, since its conventions organize most other constituents, in a subtly expressive way. . . . It need hardly be said that the limiting genre is the state of the genre at the time when the work was written.
>
> (Fowler 1982: 256)[1]

It is in the phase of interpretation, which should proceed only when 'the construction corresponds as far as possible to the intended original', that the critical reader goes beyond the 'then-meaning' of the text and discusses its significance in the context of the different interests and assumptions of the present day. But, following Hirsch, Fowler insists that 'part of the experience of an old work is precisely a sense of its distance, its alterity', so that a valid interpretation must include that 'original meaning', which 'depends upon identification of signals in terms of conventions shared with the author' (Fowler 1982: 263, 268-9).

The foregoing overview of Fowler's work and of various branches of modern linguistic and literary theory reflected in it may serve to indicate the extent to which genre criticism as a theoretical approach has been rehabilitated in recent years. For the practical purpose of reading specific texts, however, it is necessary to have an organized descriptive analysis of the individual types of literary work that constitute the universe of literature – whether that universe is conceived synchronically according to the neoclassical model (as a system of fundamental genres that persists through time or exists in an ideal form beyond the temporal) or diachronically along the lines elaborated by modern theorists (as a changing set of variables that cohere in particular formations for periods of limited duration). It is because they have proved to be eminently usable in the construction and interpretation of individual texts that aspects of the system elaborated in Northrop Frye's *Anatomy of Criticism* (1957) have been selected to provide the main point of departure for a generic approach to *Antony and Cleopatra* in this chapter.

The four essays that make up *Anatomy of Criticism* are historically significant as the first modern attempt to explore 'the possibility of a synoptic view of the scope, theory, principles, and techniques of literary criticism' (Frye 1957: 3). Frye (1957: 14) endorses Aristotle's belief 'that there is a totally intelligible structure of knowledge attainable about poetry which is not poetry itself, or the experience of it, but poetics', and, taking his cue from the Greek pioneer of the systematic analysis of literature, he establishes what Hernadi (1972: 145) calls 'a polycentric conceptual framework'. Aristotle had identified three fundamental respects in which one literary artefact could be seen to differ from another: the expressive medium (prose, verse, different metrical forms); the objects represented (characters and actions); and the manner of representation (lyric, narrative or drama). Frye's scheme consists of four related but distinct sets of theoretical criteria for the classification of literary works. In the first essay, entitled 'Historical Criticism: Theory of Modes', he argues that literary fictions can be classified according to the nature and status of the hero, who may be presented as superior, equal or inferior to the reader in kind or degree; he then goes on to differentiate broadly between tragic modes, comic modes and thematic modes, and more narrowly between various species of tragic, comic and thematic composition. The second essay, 'Ethical Criticism: Theory of Symbols', defines the word 'symbol' as 'any unit of any literary structure that can be isolated for critical attention' (Frye 1957: 71), and explains that such units, from the single word or image to larger patterns of action or imagery, can be read for 'a variety or sequence of meanings' (Frye 1957: 72), running from the literal and descriptive phases of symbolism by way of the formal and archetypal to the universal. The third essay, 'Archetypal Criticism: Theory of Myths', seeks to establish 'a grammar of literary archetypes' based on the premise that the structural principles of literature are 'closely related to mythology and comparative religion' (Frye 1957: 134–5); four classes of literature are distinguished – the romantic, the tragic, the comic, and the ironic or satiric – which are 'broader than, or logically prior to, the ordinary literary genres', and each of these '*mythoi* or generic plots' (Frye 1957: 162) is associated with one of the four seasons. Turning in the fourth essay, 'Rhetorical Criticism: Theory of Genres', to Aristotle's categories of lyric, narrative and drama, Frye develops his own fourfold method of defining genres according to their 'radical of presentation', that is, whether they are designed ideally to be acted in front of a spectator, spoken in front of a listener, sung or chanted, or read from the printed page.

In a 'Polemical Introduction' to *Anatomy of Criticism*, Frye insists on the exploratory nature of his book, which has no claim to the status of a fully worked-out and rigid system or theory: 'It is to be regarded rather as an interconnected group of suggestions which it is hoped will be of some practical use to critics and students of literature. Whatever is of no practical use to anybody is expendable' (Frye 1957: 3). His objective was to create a conceptual framework for the study of literature by uncovering and schematizing, through an appeal to myths and archetypes recognized as part of a common classical and Christian heritage, some of the deep structures that can be observed in the recurring narrative patterns, character-types, and organizing metaphors of

Western literary traditions. And in fact, there is plenty of evidence in the critical output of the past 30 years that Frye's descriptions of the structures and conventions of tragedy, comedy, romance and satire have been particularly productive in relation to the drama of Shakespeare and his contemporaries.[2] This is because it has become increasingly apparent, through the work of Rosalie Colie and other scholars, that 'the notion of genre' was historically significant 'as an expression of Renaissance culture' (Colie 1973: 2). Indeed, so central were the 'resources of kind' to the literary perceptions of Shakespeare's time that Orgel (1979: 123) can conclude an essay on Shakespeare's generic practice with the following observations on *Measure for Measure*:

> Shakespeare could make such a play effective and the spectators could respond to it because they believed in the living reality of the dramatic genres. The categories were not only what related the culture to its past but also what related the playwright and his audience to one another. Like Scaliger, Shakespeare thought of genres not as sets of rules but as sets of expectations and possibilities. Comedy and tragedy were not forms: they were shared assumptions.

In response to Frye's own invitation to extract only what may be of practical value from the rich mine of suggestions in his book, the groundwork for the critical tasks of construction and interpretation ahead of us can best be laid by identifying those features of his descriptive analysis of the universe of literature which can be shown to shed light on the 'sets of expectations and possibilities' activated by the text of *Antony and Cleopatra*. For this particular purpose, the first and third essays have a good many insights to offer and it is on these that I shall concentrate. The first thing to notice is that their arguments are largely elaborated from Aristotle's classification of genres according to the kinds of *characters* and *actions* that they represent: Frye's five modes of fiction are distinguished 'by the different elevations of the characters in them' (Frye 1957: 33); and his four basic myths are the 'narrative pregeneric elements' (Frye 1957: 162) which lie behind the plots of individual works of literature.

Since a good deal of critical debate revolves around an interpretation of Antony and Cleopatra themselves, it will be useful to look more closely at Frye's character-based categories. At the top of his scale is the mode of *myth*, in which the hero is a divine being, superior in *kind* to ordinary men and to the environment. Next comes the hero of the mode of *romance*, who is superior in *degree* to other men and to his environment, but who – although he can perform marvellous feats which transcend the normal laws of nature – is not himself super-natural. Below this, the hero of the *high mimetic* mode is superior in degree to other men, but is 'subject both to social criticism and to the order of nature' (Frye 1957: 34). The hero of the *low mimetic* mode is on a level with his readers, superior neither to other men nor to his environment. At the bottom of the scale is the hero of the *ironic* mode, who is inferior in power or intelligence to his readers. Frye (1957: 35) then sets up a contrast between *tragic* fictions, 'in which the hero becomes isolated from his society', and *comic* fictions, 'in which he is incorporated into it'. By applying this distinction to the hierarchy of modes, he is able to identify different categories of tragedy: 'tragedy in the central or high mimetic sense', involving the figure of a leader 'balanced midway between godlike heroism and all-too-human irony', whose fall generates pity and fear; and 'low mimetic or domestic tragedy', whose hero, 'isolated by a weakness which appeals to our sympathy because it is on our own level of experience', excites merely pathos (Frye 1957: 37–8). Similar insights are gained by differentiating the high mimetic Old Comedy of Aristophanes from the low mimetic New Comedy of Plautus and Terence: in the former 'there is usually a central figure who constructs his own society in the teeth of strong opposition, driving off one after another all the people who come to prevent or exploit him, and eventually achieving a heroic triumph' (Frye 1957: 43); and in the latter, after an erotic intrigue which is resolved by a twist in the plot, 'a new society crystallizes on the stage around the hero and his bride' (Frye 1957: 44). Shakespeare developed the New Comedy type in a high mimetic direction, and his comedies of romantic courtship usually dramatize a struggle between two worlds, one like our own or worse and the other enchanted or idyllic. It is also worth remembering that the modes and the hero-types they derive from do not necessarily occur in isolation in specific literary works, but are often found in combina-tion. 'For while one mode constitutes the underlying tonality of a work of fiction, any or all of the other four may be simultaneously present. Much of our sense of the subtlety of great literature comes from this modal counterpoint' (Frye 1957: 50–51).

Fundamental to Frye's approach to classification in terms of *mythoi* or generic narratives is the idea of *displacement*, the process by which the 'abstract fictional designs' or simple story structures of myth are developed in the direction of verisimilitude and plausibility, so that the work of literature presents us with 'human experience skilfully and consistently imitated' (Frye 1957: 135). The movement down the scale of fictional modes is thus from the abstract and conventionalized world of myth by way of the idealizing tendencies of romance towards the increasingly extreme realism of the low mimetic and the ironic. The aim of archetypal criticism in the third essay is to recover the underlying structures of myth that have been concealed by displacement in the interests of lifelike representation. As an example, Frye cites the way in which the abstract design of death and revival is slightly displaced in the classical myth of Proserpine, who disappears for six months of the year into the underworld and whose annual return heralds the approach of spring. This same 'structural element' is found in a number of Shakespeare's comedies, 'where it has to be adapted to a roughly high mimetic level of credibility' (Frye 1957: 138): Hero in *Much Ado About Nothing*, Imogen in *Cymbeline*, and Perdita in *The Winter's Tale* are all given up for dead and two of them even receive funeral obsequies before their restoration seals the happy ending in their respective plays.

Of the four broad narrative categories that Frye goes on to examine in detail, his first contrasting pair of comedy and tragedy are of importance for *Antony and Cleopatra*. He begins his account of comedy by pointing out that in its dramatic form many of the structural principles and character types found in the works of Aristophanes and Plautus have persisted down to our own time. The plot of a comedy tends to dramatize a movement from illusion to reality, and this will involve the transition 'from a society controlled by habit, ritual bondage, arbitrary law and the older characters to a society controlled by youth and pragmatic freedom' (Frye 1957: 169). This means that comedy often has a subversive quality, which can be felt as a threat to conventional values. The hero, who challenges the habits and laws upheld by the authority figures of his community, usually represents the younger generation, and the obstacles placed in his path form the action of the play. His triumph over the guardians of the old order supplies the comic resolution, which is frequently brought about by a reversal in the plot, and the emergence of a new social order is signalled by communal festivities. In the plot structure that Shakespeare inherited from classical New Comedy, the young hero meets opposition to his desire for a young woman, overcomes it eventually by means of a device, and becomes the centre of a new society symbolized by the ceremony of betrothal or marriage. A crucial element in this narrative structure is the moment of comic discovery or *anagnorisis*, which occurs at the point of resolution in the action and which may be effected by the removal of disguise, the recognition of kinship, or the unexpected return of a character presumed dead. Frye (1957: 170) sums up the final impact of the traditional plot of comedy:

'Happy endings do not impress us as true, but as desirable, and they are brought about by manipulation'.

Just as the five modes of Frye's analysis are arranged on a vertical scale, so his four *mythoi* are arranged in a pattern based on the rotation of the seasons, from spring (comedy), through summer (romance) and autumn (tragedy), to winter (irony and satire). Each *mythos* contains six phases, three of which are associated with the *mythos* on one side and three with the *mythos* on the other side in the seasonal cycle. Thus, a comedy will have more or less connection with the adjacent *mythos* of irony or of romance. The traditional New Comedy model is located in one of the ironic phases of the cycle, whereas Shakespeare's adaptation of the erotic intrigue plot belongs on the romantic side. Frye (1957: 182) labels this Shakespearian type 'the drama of the green world' and summarizes the design of its plot: 'Thus the action of the comedy begins in a world represented as a normal world, moves into the green world, goes into a metamorphosis there in which the comic resolution is achieved, and returns to the normal world'. The basic comic contest between youth and age, pragmatic freedom and arbitrary law, can take a more complex form in which the green world has analogies 'not only to the fertile world of ritual, but to the dream world that we create out of our own desire'. In such plays as *A Midsummer Night's Dream*, *As You Like It* and *The Winter's Tale*, the dream world 'collides with the stumbling and blinded follies of the world of experience . . . and yet proves strong enough to impose the form of desire on it' (Frye 1957: 183–4).

Like Aristotle, Frye insists that the source of tragic effect must be sought not in the personality of the hero but in the structure of the plot. The fundamental action of tragedy originates in some act of provocation committed by the hero, which is felt as a violation of natural law and which 'sets up an antithetical or counterbalancing movement' (Frye 1957: 209). The righting of the balance was called *nemesis* by the Greeks, and whether it is carried out by human or divine agency, by accident, fate, or the logic of events, 'the essential thing is that *nemesis* happens, and happens impersonally, unaffected, as *Oedipus Tyrannus* illustrates, by the moral quality of human motivation involved' (Frye 1957: 209). The act which sets the tragic machine in motion may be attributed to an external fate or to a flaw (Aristotle's *hamartia*) in the hero. But even if the majority of tragic heroes do possess *hybris* – 'a proud, passionate, obsessed or soaring mind which brings about a morally intelligible downfall' – the disaster which overwhelms them is still felt to involve 'some far-reaching mystery of which this morally intelligible process is only a part' (Frye 1957: 210–11). The action of a tragedy will lead to a crucial moment 'from which point the road to what might have been and the road to what will be can be simultaneously seen', and after which 'the wheel of fortune begins its inevitable cyclical movement downward' (Frye 1957: 213). The resolution of the tragic plot (Aristotle's *catastrophe*) often encompasses the death of the hero and is precipitated by a discovery which

> is not simply the knowledge by the hero of what has happened to him . . . but the recognition of the determined shape of the life he has created for himself, with an implicit comparison with the uncreated potential life he has forsaken.
>
> (Frye 1957: 212)

The six phases of tragedy acording to Frye's cyclical model reach out towards irony in one direction and romance in the other. In the romantic phases of tragedy, the heroic elements in the central character are emphasized; in the ironic phases are placed the fall of the hero through *hybris* and *hamartia* and 'the tragedy of lost direction and lack of knowledge' (Frye 1957: 222).

Since love was commonly material for comedy rather than for tragedy in Shakespearian drama, Frye's gloss on the narrative consequences of highlighting the sexual dimension of human behaviour in the two genres may conveniently serve to bring this brief account of his critical system to a close and to open the way for an analysis of Shakespeare's treatment of one of the great love stories of the Western world:

> In comedy the erotic and social affinities of the hero are combined and unified in the final scene; tragedy usually makes love and the social structure irreconcilable and contending forces, a conflict which reduces love to passion and social activity to a forbidding and imperative duty.
>
> (Frye 1957: 218)

II

Three times in the opening speech of *Antony and Cleopatra*, Philo asserts the destructive influence of sexual passion on the general he once admired: the 'goodly eyes' (I.i.2) of the Mars-like Antony now bend their view 'Upon a tawny front' (I.i.6); his 'captain's heart' (I.i.6) has become 'the bellows and the fan/To cool a gipsy's lust' (I.i.9–10); and the man whose duty has called him to be 'the triple pillar of the world' is 'transformed/Into a strumpet's fool' (I.i.12–13). For

Philo, and for the critical tradition that endorses his view of the action that follows, this is a play about the conflict between love and duty in the life of the hero: it is essentially the tragedy of Antony.[3] But the full title, as it was first printed in the 1623 Folio of Shakespeare's works, indicates a different 'frame of reference' (Jauss 1970: 11) for those reader's 'expectations' upon which contemporary theories of interpretation place such importance. *The Tragedy of Antony and Cleopatra* announces not only a broad affiliation to the tragic genre but also membership of a specialized subcategory, which has been distinguished from other kinds of tragedy by its orchestration of 'an ending in which two characters separately yet jointly undergo tragic downfalls and deaths' (Rozett 1985: 152). The combination of an action motivated by sexual love and a dramatic emphasis that falls equally on the hero and the heroine (like *Romeo and Juliet*, but unlike *Othello*, in which the death of Desdemona is the climactic event in the tragedy of the isolated hero) is presumably what makes it 'decidedly different' for Bradley from the single-protagonist plays. Indeed, the first scene quickly makes it clear that Philo's perspective is not the only one from which to interpret the relationship between the Roman general and the Egyptian queen, and another critical tradition has found the key to the text's meaning not in the carping of the Roman observer, but in the hero's declaration of love's transcendent value:

> Let Rome in Tiber melt, and the wide arch
> Of the ranged empire fall! . . .
> . . . The nobleness of life
> Is to do thus, [*embracing Cleopatra*] when such a mutual pair
> And such a twain can do't . . .
>
> (I.i.35–6, 38–40)

Traversi (1963: 79) speaks of the impasse in which students of *Antony and Cleopatra* sooner or later find themselves, 'faced by two possible readings of the play, whose only difficulty is that they seem to be mutually exclusive'. In terms of Frye's system of classification, the choice is between locating it within one of the ironic phases of tragedy as the fall of a leader who gave up his empire to a whore and locating it within one of the romantic phases of tragedy as a drama of the world well lost for love.

To find a way out of this impasse, it is necessary to go back to the 'construction' stage of Fowler's programme for critical reading and try to determine 'the features of the work' with as much accuracy as possible. Bearing in mind both his claim that genre 'can be a powerful instrument' in this endeavour and Frye's reminder that much of the subtlety of great literature comes from 'modal counterpoint', we might begin by recognizing that the play exhibits features of more than one literary kind, which point in different directions and elicit contradictory responses and judgements. Colie (1974: 5) sees this as characteristic of the art of an age in which 'there was an insistence on outdoing and overgoing earlier achievements, each man newly creating out of and against his tradition, in conscious competition with the very best that tradition could offer him'. Citing *Hamlet* and *The Winter's Tale* as examples of Shakespeare's particular boldness and ingenuity in this respect, she describes them as 'mixtures of genres – *two* invitations to form issued at once' (Colie 1974: 9). This is merely to acknowledge, in terms of modern theory, what Dr Samuel Johnson had noticed at the height of the neoclassical period in the preface to his 1765 edition of Shakespeare's works: 'Shakespeare's plays are not in the rigorous and critical sense either tragedies or comedies, but compositions of a distinct kind'. Explaining the rise of tragedy and comedy in the ancient world as literary types 'intended to promote different ends by contrary means', he proclaims himself unable to 'recollect among the *Greeks* or *Romans* a single writer who attempted both', and adds:

> Shakespeare has united the powers of exciting laughter and sorrow not only in one mind but in one composition. Almost all his plays are divided between serious and ludicrous characters, and, in the successive evolutions of the design, sometimes produce seriousness and sorrow, and sometimes levity and laughter.
>
> (Johnson 1986: 14–15)

At its simplest, Shakespeare's mingling of tragic and comic elements is a matter of introducing one of the Company clowns to provide a brief respite from the oppressiveness of the tragic atmosphere, as when the murder of Duncan is followed by an interlude with a drunken porter in *Macbeth*. More complex are instances of major figures in a tragic plot involving themselves in comic performances, such as the Prince of Denmark's adoption of the role of jester, which leads Johnson to comment that the 'pretended madness of Hamlet causes much mirth' (Johnson 1986: 344). The same process operates in reverse, when comedies are darkened by tragic overtones. In *The Merchant of Venice*, for example, Shylock ceases to be a figure of fun when he demands his pound of flesh, and he even excites pity when he is finally humiliated and driven from the stage. More complex still are those plays which

defy definition in terms of a dominant genre and effect a major structural shift from one to another in 'the successive evolutions of the
design'. In such cases, as Colie (1974: 16) notes, the 'generic associations' are usually 'clearly marked'.

Measure for Measure develops an
intractable situation in the first two and a half acts, with all the
psychological realism and intensity of Shakespeare's tragic manner; but
the Duke of Vienna in his disguise as a friar begins to meddle in the
plot, importing implausible devices from the genre of romance and
bringing Act III to a close with a chant-like speech in rhyming
couplets, in which he reassures us that a comic outcome is now to
be expected. *The Winter's Tale* similarly pursues what seems to be a
tragic course until the last scene of Act III, when romantic conventions
decisively break the generic mould; and at the start of Act IV, Time
enters as Chorus to announce that he both 'makes and unfolds error'
(IV.i.2) and to prepare us for the very different dramatic methods of
pastoral comedy which dominate the last two acts. The play which
is in some ways nearest to Shakespeare's manipulation of the resources
of genre in *Antony and Cleopatra* is *Romeo and Juliet*, the other love
tragedy with a double focus on hero and heroine. The situation
presented in Acts I and II contains many of the ingredients of
comedy, but the deaths of Tybalt and Mercutio at the beginning of
Act III divert the action towards a tragic climax, and the feigned death
of Juliet – a traditionally comic device masterminded by one of
Shakespeare's well-meaning friars – goes disastrously wrong.[4]

If we turn again to the opening scene of *Antony and Cleopatra*, and
resume the task of constructing it from the signals sent out by the
text, we can see that certain features are at odds with the tragic expectations created by Philo's critical comments and Antony's romantic
exaltation of 'such a mutual pair' (I.i.39). Messengers from Rome,
together with references to the 'powerful mandate' (I.i.23) of Caesar,
the taking in and enfranchising of kingdoms, and Cleopatra's position
as 'Egypt's queen' (I.i.31), locate this pair of lovers in a political context where much more is at stake than their own lives and happiness.
In contrast to the woeful story of Juliet and her Romeo, whose private
tragedy was confined to the domestic realm, the fate of 'such a twain'
(I.i.40) as Antony and Cleopatra cannot be extricated from that of 'the
wide arch/Of the ranged empire' (I.i.35–6). Every move they make
is a matter of public consequence and food for the 'common liar' in
Rome (I.i.62). These are the marks of a work that is best designated
by 'the new generic term, "history" – a term under which a third of
Shakespeare's plays were printed in the First Folio' (Nicoll 1960–61:
84). Frye (1957: 283–4) argues that this new dramatic kind evolved

out of the earlier Scripture-based 'myth-play' to serve the secular ends of the Tudor state: 'The central theme of Elizabethan history is the unifying of the nation and the binding of the audience into the myth as the inheritors of that unity, set over against the disasters of civil war and weak leadership'; and he adds that in dramatizations of the English chronicles in plays such as *Richard II* and *Richard III*, 'history merges so gradually into tragedy that we often cannot be sure when communion has turned into catharsis'. In *Julius Caesar*, the play which was written soon after the completion of Shakespeare's second tetralogy of plays about the dynastic rivalries of the fifteenth century, Roman history permitted a more objective exploration of the nature of civil war and the struggle for political power. North's translation of Plutarch, the main source for *Antony and Cleopatra*, took the story beyond the deaths of Brutus and Cassius to the significant moment when Octavius became the 'sole sir o' the world' (V.ii.120) and presided over a 'time of universal peace' (IV.vi.4) as the emperor Augustus.

The extraordinarily rich 'modal counterpoint' of this play, however, does not merely offer an invitation to experience another gradual merging of history into tragedy, as in *Richard II* or *Julius Caesar*. If we accept Philo's injunction to 'Take but good note' (I.i.11) of the first encounter between Antony and Cleopatra, we become aware of features that belong to a third kind of dramatic tradition. Casting her lover in the roles of obsequious servant to 'the scarce-bearded Caesar' (I.i.22) and henpecked husband of 'shrill-tongued Fulvia' (I.i.34), Cleopatra's playful mockery has more in common with the 'merry war' of words between Benedick and Beatrice in *Much Ado About Nothing* than with the sober worlds of tragedy and history. The battle of the sexes had been at the centre of Shakespeare's vision in a long string of comedies in the 1590s and even *Romeo and Juliet* had to tear itself free of comic conventions and attitudes in order to pursue its tragic purpose. As Frye (1957: 181) points out, '[t]he presiding genius of comedy is Eros'; and in the essentially comic world of Cleopatra's Egypt, love and sensuality reign supreme. But in the carnival atmosphere that she creates around her, even love is not safe from her mischievous delight in deflating the grandeur of its rhetoric.[5] She eggs Antony on to extravagant expressions of his devotion to her: 'There's beggary in the love that can be reckoned' (I.i.15). But a few lines later, when he rejects the Roman – and history's – emphasis on political and military power and commits himself wholeheartedly to the Egyptian – and comedy's – elevation of romantic love as the highest value in life, she undermines the splendour of his declaration ('We stand up peerless') with a teasing reply ('Excellent falsehood!'

(I.i.42)), and plunges straight into a witty proof that they are both little better than fools. So Philo is not entirely wrong about Antony's becoming 'a strumpet's fool'. But his view can only be accepted as entirely right by an audience that refuses the invitation to respond *both* to the poetry of love's magnificent excess, *and* to the fascination of Cleopatra's playful debunking of that excess, and so confines itself to the grim perspective which judges everything by the criterion of practical success in war and politics.

At this juncture, an overview of *Antony and Cleopatra* will be necessary, to provide a framework for showing how the genres of tragedy, comedy and history contrast and fuse with each other in a complex design. Johnson had differentiated the Elizabethan history play from the other two kinds of drama by its lack of elaborate plot: 'History was a series of actions, with no other than chronological succession, independent on each other, and without any tendency to introduce or regulate the conclusion' (Johnson 1986: 16). The basis of Shakespeare's dramatic structure is certainly the series of historical events recorded by Plutarch: the tensions that beset the triumvirate after their defeat of Brutus at the battle of Philippi; the 'garboils' and death of Fulvia; the temporary truce between Antony and Caesar, sealed by the marriage to Octavia; the settlement with Sextus Pompey and his subsequent murder; the military success of Antony's lieutenant, Ventidius, against the Parthians; Antony's return to Egypt and the rift with Caesar, which led to a fresh outbreak of civil war and culminated in Caesar's victory at the battle of Actium; and the suicides of Antony and Cleopatra. Upon these foundations of history, Shakespeare erected a dramatic edifice out of conventions derived from both tragedy and comedy. In some respects, it is similar to the structure of *Romeo and Juliet*, *Measure for Measure*, and *The Winter's Tale* described earlier, in which a transition from one dominant genre to another is clearly marked. Here, the comic perspective is in the ascendency until a 'crucial moment' half-way through Act III, after which 'the wheel of fortune begins its inevitable cyclical movement downward' (Frye 1957: 213) and tragedy assumes control over both the plot and the perspective from which it is viewed. *Antony and Cleopatra* is further complicated, however, by the presence of the competing values of history and by a disruption of generic decorum, when the traditional tragic conclusion, 'in which the hero becomes isolated from his society', has to be adjusted to accommodate the comic conclusion, 'in which he is incorporated into it' (Frye 1957: 35).

At the heart of the play's comic life is the figure of Cleopatra. Her festive gaiety opposes and subverts the seriousness of history

represented in its strictest form by Octavius Caesar, who sneers at
Antony's 'lascivious wassails' (I.iv.56) and is shocked at the thought
that his partner in empire should 'tumble on the bed of Ptolemy'
(I.iv.17). One of Shakespeare's boldest innovations is to reverse the
familiar age profile of comedy, and invest 'the boy Caesar' with the
guardianship of law and convention against the challenge mounted by
the passion of a lover with a 'grizzled head' (III.xiii.17) and a woman
who is 'wrinkled deep in time' (I.v.29). Like Falstaff – the embodiment of the carnival values which compete against honour and justice
for the allegiance of Prince Hal in the *Henry IV* plays – Cleopatra
constructs her own society in the teeth of respectable morality in the
manner of an Old Comedy heroine; and her palace in Alexandria,
where she holds court like the fat knight in the Eastcheap tavern, is
one of those 'dream world' extensions of the Shakespearian 'green
world' of romantic comedy which can 'impose the form of desire' upon
the 'blinded follies of the world of experience' (Frye 1957: 183–4) – that
world governed by fortune in which it is 'paltry to be Caesar'. In the
first scene, Antony's immersion in the holiday mood of Egypt is total:

> There's not a minute of our lives should stretch
> Without some pleasure now. What sport tonight?
>
> (I.i.48–9).

When he is away in Rome, Cleopatra recalls how he once gave himself
up to the uninhibited mirth of her Feast of Misrule:

> That time? O times!
> I laughed him out of patience, and that night
> I laughed him into patience, and next morn,
> Ere the ninth hour, I drunk him to his bed . . .
>
> (II.v.18–21)

The third scene demonstrates the quality in which, more than
anything else, lies the secret of Cleopatra's 'infinite variety': a love of
play-acting she shares with Falstaff. As soon as Antony enters, she is
'sick and sullen' (I.iii.13). The next moment, she adopts the role of
the victim of infidelity, whose man is being lured away by another
woman – 'I have no power upon you; hers you are' (I.iii.23) – though
in this case, the performance is mischievously undercut by the
knowledge that the other woman is Antony's lawful wife. After being
thrown off balance for a moment by the news that Fulvia is dead, she
resumes her teasing provocation of Antony by urging him to weep
for his wife and pretend that the tears are being shed because he must
leave Egypt:

> Good now, play one scene
> Of excellent dissembling, and let it look
> Like perfect honour.
>
> (I.iii.78–80)

These lines open up a central problem that the comic dimension of this play poses for its audiences: if the dissembling is excellent enough, how can the simulated emotion be distinguished from the real thing? In the creative 'dream world' of Cleopatra, performance is all, and a part played with skill and energy may call into existence an imaginative order of being that offers a challenge to the dull orthodoxies of morality and history, in which wives have more legitimate claims than mistresses and love has to give way to 'The strong necessity of time' (I.iii.42).

After this scene, the focus of dramatic action shifts from the pleasures of Egypt to the business of Rome. But Shakespeare does not encourage us to take his Roman statesmen and generals exclusively at their own – or history's – evaluation. Various devices are employed to ensure that the irreverent perspective of comedy continues to colour our response to the preoccupations of empire: short scenes in Alexandria keep the queen's uninhibited displays of passion directly before the audience; Enobarbus imports the comic spirit into the central arena of politics with those 'light answers' (I.ii.175) which irritate Antony in his serious mood; and his sceptical commentary persistently undermines the solemnity of the power-games in Rome. The dividing line between dignity and pomposity is a narrow one, and comedy in its ironic modes specializes in ridiculing the inflated images with which authority figures seek to maintain their self-esteem. Beneath the pageant of Roman history in the first half of the play runs an undercurrent of mockery, ready to break the surface whenever we let the spirit of mischief direct our perception of the priggishness of so many of Caesar's utterances, the hollow complacency of Pompey, the drunken ineptitude of Lepidus, and the cynical expediency of Antony's marriage. The long series of political manœuvres comes to a climax when Octavia returns 'A market-maid to Rome' (III.vi.51), in a scene which constitutes the crucial turning-point in Antony's career and modulates the dominant tone of the play from comedy to tragedy.

In the portrait of Antony created during the first half of the play, there have been hints of the romance hero who can transcend the limits of nature: even Caesar retails his legendary achievements as a leader of men when he says, 'On the Alps/It is reported thou didst eat strange flesh,/Which some did die to look on' (I.iv.66–8); Pompey admits that 'his soldiership/Is twice the other twain' (II.i.34–5); and as Cleopatra's lover he has 'O'erflow[ed] the measure' (I.i.2) with an extravagance beyond the appreciation of ordinary men like Philo. Up to this point, in his period of prosperity, he has contrived to exercise both the Roman and the Egyptian dimensions of his character by keeping them apart. The antithetical movement of *nemesis* which will bring him to his death is not, as the prim Caesar would have it, provoked by the moral crime of his adulterous liaison with Egypt's queen, but by the *hybris* of his attempt to claim for himself the contradictory prizes of supreme love and supreme power in this world. It is this act of over-reaching – this refusal to be bound in service to the 'strong necessity of time' – that throws out a challenge to the natural law which human beings transgress at their peril. From this moment on, Antony will demonstrate that his heroic (high mimetic mode) qualities do not exempt him from the order of nature and, in the eyes of both foes and followers, he will even sink to the bottom of Frye's scale of heroic types and be regarded with irony as nothing more than an 'old ruffian' (IV.i.4) or 'a doting mallard' (III.x.19). The Soothsayer had earlier struck the note of portending tragedy in his warning to Antony about the folly of a direct contest with Caesar. Now, Caesar is quick to cast himself in the role of divine avenger of his sister's honour:

> You are abused
> Beyond the mark of thought; and the high god,
> To do you justice, makes his ministers
> Of us ...
>
> (III.vi.87–90)

He also assumes the role of fate's agent in the coming showdown. Echoing Antony's earlier words, he advises Octavia not to let 'these strong necessities' trouble her, but to accept the unfolding of events to their ordained conclusion: 'But let determined things to destiny/ Hold unbewailed their way' (III.vi.84–6).

This double invocation of the 'high god' and 'destiny' evokes that sense of mystery – introduced by the Soothsayer and later reinforced by the strange music that marks the departure of 'the god Hercules' (IV.iii.14) – which accompanies the morally intelligible aspects of the tragic process; and it helps to alter the audience's attitude to the antics of the politicians, as the comic mood of the play is displaced by the tragic. In the next scene, the note of foreboding deepens, when Antony takes his reckless decision to fight at sea against the ominous accumulation of advice from Camidius, Enobarbus and an anonymous soldier. The shameful defeat at Actium is recorded in a series of brief scenes, and within 50 lines the foundations of the carnival world of Egypt have been destroyed, Antony has given way to despair, and the stage is set for the inevitable progress towards the death of the hero that brings the plot of a tragedy to its formal close.

In this transitional phase of the play, as a prelude and foil to the double climax that is to crown the central tragedy of love, a complication is added to the design with the emergence of Enobarbus from his role of plain-speaker to become the central figure in a subsidiary tragic action. When Antony's men begin to fall away, Enobarbus decides – against his better judgement – to remain loyal. By the end of Act III, however, Antony's folly and doubts about Cleopatra's fidelity have brought him to the crucial decision from which there can be no turning back: 'I will seek/Some way to leave him' (III.xiii.200–1). Fast on the heels of his defection, Antony sends his treasure after him and Enobarbus's eyes are opened to the true nature of his former master and to his own unredeemable guilt. This moment of discovery (*anagnorisis*) follows precisely the model described by Frye, in which the tragic hero recognizes 'the determined shape of the life he has created for himself' and compares it with 'the uncreated potential life he has forsaken' (Frye 1957: 212):

> I am alone the villain of the earth,
> And feel I am so most. O Anthony,
> Thou mine of bounty, how wouldst thou have paid
> My better service, when my turpitude
> Thou dost so crown with gold!
>
> (IV.vi.29–33)

The catastrophe of this minor tragic action occurs four short scenes later, when he has sought out 'Some ditch wherein to die' (IV.vi.37). Calling upon the moon as 'sovereign mistress of true melancholy' (IV.x.12), he expires with the name of the leader he has deserted on his lips and brings to a suitably pathetic conclusion the low mimetic tragedy of a man whose weakness 'appeals to our sympathy' (Frye 1957: 38) rather than exciting the pity and fear of the high mimetic mode.

As the inexorable process of Antony's isolation begins, most painfully dramatized in Enobarbus's defection, so the tragic theme of individual identity rises into prominence. 'Had our general/Been what he knew himself,' says Camidius, 'it had gone well' (III.x.25–6). The question of Antony's true self has always been latent in the play. But in the aftermath of Actium, the issue of which is his *truest* self – the great protagonist in the drama of world history or the great lover for whom 'Kingdoms are clay' (I.i.37) – becomes an urgent one for the hero himself. It is raised acutely by the desertion of Cleopatra's fleet in the final battle: 'Betrayed I am./O this false soul of Egypt!' (IV.xiii.24–5), cries Antony; and in this moment of bitter discovery, he comes to a decision that looks as if it will lead to an Othello-like resolution of his pain: 'To the young Roman boy she hath sold me, and I fall/Under this plot – she dies for't' (IV.xiii.48–9). Very soon, the unstable shapes of the clouds in the evening sky – 'black vesper's pageants' (IV.xv.8) – have led him to contemplate his uncertain grip upon his own identity: 'I made these wars for Egypt, and the Queen – /Whose heart I thought I had, for she had mine' (IV.xv.15–16). If the queen is false, then his whole life has been based on a lie and his sense of himself as Antony the lover of Cleopatra dissolves like a cloud, and becomes 'indistinct/As water is in water' (IV.xv.10–11). Mardian's report that Cleopatra has killed herself induces a second moment of discovery, which cancels the earlier one and resolves Antony's dilemma. If she died for love of him, repeating his name, then his identity as lover is vindicated and he can put aside that other self: 'No more a soldier. Bruisèd pieces, go,/You have been nobly borne' (IV.xv.42–3). He recognizes 'the determined shape of the life he has created for himself', approves it (in contrast to Enobarbus), and prepares to perform the deed that will both confirm him in the role that expresses the deepest needs of his nature and satisfy the finest values of the other side of his experience: 'a Roman, by a Roman/ Valiantly vanquished' (IV.xvi.59–60).

The affirmation of the undefeated self is the climactic event in the higher modes of the tragic vision of life, but in this hero's ceremony of dying another dramatic rhythm can be discerned, which derives from comedy rather than tragedy. Looking beyond the isolation of death to the perfected relationship which is the goal of the comic plot, he imagines that he and Cleopatra will wander for ever 'hand in hand,/ And with our sprightly port make the ghosts gaze' (IV.xv.51–2). From the perspective of this ending, the play's action can be viewed as a movement away from the 'habit, ritual bondage, arbitrary law' of the society over which Caesar exerts his rule towards the 'pragmatic freedom' (Frye 1957: 169) of a new society beyond the grave, which – after all the vicissitudes that beset the course of true love in the New Comedy plot – will 'crystallize . . . around the hero and his bride' (Frye 1957: 44). It is entirely appropriate that Antony's imagery mingles the climactic rites of tragedy and comedy a few lines later: 'But I will be/A bridegroom in my death, and run into't/As to a lover's bed' (IV.xv.99–101). There is yet another discovery or twist of the plot, based on the Proserpine myth of death and return that effects the resolution in several of Shakespeare's romantic comedies, when Antony learns that Cleopatra's suicide was one more piece of 'excellent dissembling' (I.iii.79). Without a word of surprise or reproach, he accepts the few precious moments afforded by this unexpected reunion and is content to lay 'Of many thousand kisses the poor last' (IV.xvi.22) upon her lips and die in her arms, having achieved his dual fulfilment as tragic and comic hero.

The question of Cleopatra's true nature and motives also takes on a different significance after the generically transitional scene of Octavia's return to Rome. The time for sport is over, and Cleopatra's rapid shifts of mood begin to look dangerously like inconstancy, deceit and betrayal, as the world of Roman politics ceases to be the target of subversive mockery and threatens the survival of the playful values of Egypt. The moment of discovery in Cleopatra's tragic career seems to coincide with Antony's death, when she recognizes that life has no further hold on her allegiance: 'there is nothing left remarkable/ Beneath the visiting moon' (IV.xvi.69–70). At the end of Act IV, she appears to have determined upon following his example:

> We'll bury him; and then, what's brave, what's noble,
> Let's do't after the high Roman fashion,
> And make death proud to take us.
>
> (IV.xvi.87–9)

But her behaviour in Act V casts doubt on this determination. Why does she tell Proculeius to inform Caesar that 'majesty, to keep decorum, must/No less beg than a kingdom' (V.ii.17–18)? Why does she seek an interview with Caesar, saying that she 'would gladly/Look him i'th'face' (V.ii.31–2)? Would she have decided to live if she had been able to make some impression upon this cold politician? And what is the truth behind the revelation by Seleucus that she has lied about her treasure and kept back items of value? The point is *not* that we should convict or acquit her of unworthy motives, but that the text does not provide sufficient evidence for us to be sure either way. The audience is brought up sharply against the impossibility of distinguishing between 'perfect honour' and 'excellent dissembling'.

As her story approaches its catastrophe, the moral distinction between dissembling and honesty ceases to matter. Faced with the certainty that she will be parodied in a Roman spectacle – that 'I shall see/Some squeaking Cleopatra boy my greatness' (V.ii.219–20) – she decides to stage her own last performance and leave the world with an image of herself that *she* has created:

> Show me, my women, like a queen. Go fetch
> My best attires. I am again for Cydnus,
> To meet Mark Anthony.
>
> (V.ii.227–9)

Of all her roles, she selects that as the final expression of her self; and her imagination is so fired by the scene that she anticipates not an end but a continuation of the relationship which she claims as the greatest reality of her experience:

> Give me my robe, put on my crown – I have
> Immortal longings in me. . . .
> . . . methinks I hear
> Anthony call; I see him rouse himself
> To praise my noble act . . .
>
> (V.ii.279–80, 282–4)

In her exalted state of mind, death itself is transformed into an aspect of sexual play – 'The stroke of death is as a lover's pinch/Which hurts, and is desired' (V.ii.294–5) – and (like Antony before her) she looks beyond the tragic resolution of her story to its comic consummation in marriage: 'Husband, I come!/Now to that name my courage prove my title!' (V.iii.286–7). She has succeeded triumphantly in imposing 'the form of desire' upon 'the world of experience' (Frye 1957: 183–4) and the audience – without needing to believe in the truth of the happy ending – basks in the desirability of her union with Antony in that comic realm of harmony, where 'souls do couch on flowers' (IV.xv.51) and 'all the haunt' (IV.xv.54) will be theirs.

Caesar is left alive to reassert the rational perspectives of history, in which the causes of death are enquired into and the appropriate public gestures are made. But the theatrical and emotional strategy of this remarkable play has contrived to satisfy all the contradictory expectations activated in its opening scene. In an exhilarating fusion of tragic and comic catastrophes, it transcends the concerns of the history play and achieves the feat of simultaneously honouring the heroism of the isolated individual and celebrating the joy of community.

III

Northrop Frye is well aware of the difference between 'criticism as a body of knowledge' about literature, which is what he sets out in *Anatomy of Criticism*, and 'the direct experience of literature, where every act is unique, and classification has no place' (Frye 1957: 29). But many critics have responded to his call to revive and develop the Aristotelian project of 'formulating the broad laws of literary experience' (Frye 1957: 14), because they are convinced of its practical application in understanding the succession of 'unique acts' that occur in the course of reading and interpreting an individual example of literary art. Fowler, who has reservations about the 'incompleteness' of Frye's scheme and about its synchronic tendency, and who acknowledges that a generic approach 'is not indeed the whole of criticism', is nevertheless certain that 'in construction it makes an invaluable contribution, by locating the work's individuality *vis-à-vis* convention' (Fowler 1982: 242–3, 262). The present chapter has been written in the belief that any 'direct experience' of *Antony and Cleopatra* (in the study or in the theatre) must bring to bear what is known about the 'generic horizon' within which the text was first created, if it is to offer anything more than a collection of subjective and historically ungrounded impressions. Since Frye's system was derived from an extensive study of 'Western literature in the context of its Classical and Christian heritage' (Frye 1957: 133) – a field in which Shakespeare's own works are themselves among the most prominent features – it has provided a useful window on to the 'set of expectations and possibilities' that constituted the 'shared assumptions' (Orgel 1979: 123) of the dramatist and his contemporary audience.

A good deal of attention has been devoted to the structure of the play, partly because both Aristotle and Frye emphasize the nature and shape of the action as a significant feature in differentiating dramatic genres, and partly because the problems of interpretation posed by *Antony and Cleopatra* have sometimes been blamed upon the looseness of its internal organization. Johnson (1986: 298) attributed this looseness to an inadequate treatment of the source material: 'The events, of which the principal are described according to history, are produced without any art of connection or care of disposition'; and Bradley (1905: 213), who considered it 'the most faultily constructed of all the tragedies', also invoked the diffusion of dramatic interest caused by the necessity, imposed by the historical facts, 'of taking frequent and fatiguing journeys over thousands of miles'. An approach through genre complexity has sought to answer such criticism by opening up to scrutiny the artful complexity of the play's structure. Without abandoning that sense of the arbitrariness of event which is an essential aspect of the play's response to its sources, it has been possible to identify the simultaneous evolutions of a comic plot (in which two lovers overcome various obstacles to their relationship and achieve final union, passing from the illusion of temporal power and bondage to history, to the emotional reality and freedom of a desired consummation in eternity) and a tragic plot (in which the hero and heroine independently rise to the challenge of asserting the value of their heroic identities against the opposition and pettiness of the mundane world). Further complexities have emerged through concentrating on such structural features as the pivotal scene of Octavia's return to Rome, which underlines the fatal error of Antony and inaugurates the shift of dominant mood from comic to tragic in the later scenes of Act III; and the climactic reversals in the careers of first Antony and then Cleopatra created by moments of discovery, which control the carefully managed oscillation between the tragic rites of self-affirmation and the comic rites of reconciliation and everlasting union. In addition, the minor tragic action centred on Enobarbus is recognized as a preparation for and foil to the catastrophe of Antony's tragedy, and its place within the kinetic design of the whole play is vindicated against negative verdicts, such as that of Mason (1970: 262), that the 'development given to Enobarbus' is merely 'a symptom of Shakespeare's failure to focus his mind'.

Emphasis has also been placed on the mixing of genres, because it is the highly sophisticated modal counterpointing in *Antony and Cleopatra* that is the cause of many of the difficulties that readers encounter, both in the initial phase of responding to the features of the text and in the subsequent phase of arranging their responses into an interpretation. For some interpreters, the heart of the problem lies in the play's refusal to provide a consistent point of view or at least give clear priority to one view over others available within the text. Whitaker (1965: 281) is representative in his complaint that 'we are left confused as to what interpretation Shakespeare wished us to place upon Antony's death, and we are even more puzzled about Cleopatra's'. The requirement that a work of literature should arrive at an unambiguous resolution derives, in fact, from the Aristotelian premises of genre theory itself, which attributed the rise of different literary kinds to the different ways in which early poets looked at human beings and their behaviour: 'The more serious-minded among them represented noble actions and the doings of noble persons, while the more trivial wrote about the meaner sort of people' (Aristotle 1965: 35–6). This explanation of the origin of genres was repeated by Johnson (1986: 14–15), in his remark that tragedy and comedy evolved in order to 'promote different ends by contrary means'; and it survives in the contemporary theory of the resources of kind in the comment that 'a genre-system offers a set of interpretations, of "frames" or "fixes" on the world' (Colie 1973: 8). What Frye and other modern exponents of genre criticism such as Colie have developed is a more sophisticated method of analysing the ways in which a writer may transgress, subvert and combine generic forms and conventions in the pursuit of more complex ends than those for which separate genres furnish the means of expression.

Antony and Cleopatra can thus be seen as a text which problematizes the tendency to allow meaning to be shaped by the generic perspective adopted by writer and reader. We have seen this happening at the level of plot conventions, when the abstract structural element of death and revival is manipulated first in the direction of tragedy (Cleopatra is dead and was faithful – the kind of discovery that Othello makes about Desdemona at the climax of his agony) and then in the direction of comedy (Cleopatra is not dead – the kind of discovery that makes possible the joyful reconciliation and reunion typical of romance). Part of Whitaker's difficulty springs from the absence of a theatrical convention established by Elizabethan dramatists as an aid to interpretation and common in earlier tragedies by Shakespeare – the authoritative revelation of motive and attitude in soliloquy. In this confusing play, the reader is 'provided no insight into the hero's own mind by which to test or interpret what others say and do' (Whitaker 1965: 280–81). The elevation of Enobarbus to tragic status half-way through the play disrupts legitimate expectations and denies the reader another conventional guide to meaning. For nearly three acts, he performs the familiar role of 'plain dealer', like Horatio in *Hamlet* or Kent in *King Lear*. Such a character, says Frye (1957: 218), is 'in the position of refusing, or at any rate resisting, the tragic movement toward catastrophe'; and, as Harris (1977: 220) points out, one of his functions as a 'discernibly reliable' commentator is to supply 'a concluding and comprehensive clarification which reveals the significance of the work's total design'. But his removal in the middle of Act IV confirms the slide towards disaster and leaves possession of the stage at the end to the spokesman for a genre which, as Frye recognizes, is antipathetic to the ritual finality of art: 'the emphasis and characteristic resolution of the history play are in terms of continuity and the closing up both of the tragic catastrophe and (as in the case of Falstaff) of the comic festival' (Frye 1957: 284). Caesar pays the necessary tributes to his dead adversaries, but explicitly cancels the vision of an eternity of love, to which the audience has just been invited to give emotional endorsement, by consigning the lovers to a 'grave upon the earth' (V.ii.357); and he places the 'solemn show' (V.ii.362) that will be put on for their funeral as one more piece of business in a crowded imperial timetable: 'And then to Rome' (V.ii.363).

That Frye is by no means unresponsive to the need to keep the historical dimension of literature in mind is quite clear in his comment that the chief flourishing of tragic drama belongs to fifth-century Athens and seventeenth-century Europe, both periods and societies 'in which an aristocracy is fast losing its effective power but still retains a good deal of ideological prestige' (Frye 1957: 37). But he is also wary of imposing 'an extra-literary schematism' upon literature, which encourages readers to see literary texts through 'a sort of religio-political color-filter' (Frye 1957: 7). He has aroused a good deal of antagonism by his consequent insistence that the literary critic's first task is 'to read literature, to make an inductive survey of his own field and let his critical principles shape themselves solely out of his knowledge of that field' (Frye 1957: 6–7). From the ideological stance of new historicism, for example, Tennenhouse (1986: 5) has claimed that the 'arrangement of plays according to generic categories auto-matically detaches the work from history' and that Frye himself has deliberately contributed to 'this great game of suppressing the political operations of writing'. I have no wish to deny the importance of recognizing that, as a Jacobean play, *Antony and Cleopatra* articulates a political adjustment to a post-Elizabethan age in which 'the iconic bond between the aristocratic female and the body politic is broken' and that it ends by 'delivering the world over to patriarchy' (Tennenhouse 1986: 144, 146). To ignore the element of formal experimentation so characteristic of Shakespeare's time and of his own practice, however, is to court the danger of granting authorial priority to one perspective among the several made available by the generic contradictions of the text. This trap is not entirely avoided in Tennenhouse's (1986: 145) argument that 'all serious threats to Rome stem from Antony's alliance with Cleopatra' and that to 'so locate the source of political disorder is to represent such disorder as pollution'. This is to give too much authority to Caesar's point of view; and to opt for an interpretation based too squarely on the values of the history play and the preoccupations of Jacobean politics is to do less than justice to the comic and tragic rhythms that make such a powerful humanistic appeal to the imagination. A reading that remains alert to the expressive resources of genre can construct a richer and more open-ended version of the play.

SUPPLEMENT

NIGEL WOOD: You quote Fowler's gloss on the 'generic horizon' of a work of art on p. 98, and seem to accept his view of genre as a powerful con-

structive principle both in authorial creation and an audience's perceptions. How would you ensure the accurate interpretation of particularly
hybrid forms where the grounds for genre recognition were not yet
formed (e.g. *The Waste Land*, or a 'problem play' such as *Troilus and
Cressida*)? Wouldn't the notion of a 'horizon' actually work against the
sympathetic reception of the radical work of art?

ROBERT WILCHER: The modern genre critic would argue that the 'radical work
of art' *is* radical by virtue of its transgression or adaptation or revival of
conventions already familiar (to the writer if not always to the reader/
audience – a point I'll come back to); and, indeed, would insist that a
literary text not written in the context of already existing literature
(created *ex nihilo* in a literary vacuum, so to speak, if such a thing were
conceivable) would be resistant to construction and interpretation,
because there would be no known landmarks (no 'generic horizon') by
which to take bearings and begin the process of reorientating ideas and
responses towards the 'newness' of the new work.

Fowler approaches the question of innovation from a number of angles.
Within a particular historical period, new sub-genres may be developed
by the process of adding special substantive features to the common
features of a kind or genre – thus the addition of the narrative topic of
blood vengeance and the associated motifs of ghosts, vows, and delays
to the emergent form of Elizabethan tragedy (which embodies the
inexorable movement of the exceptional hero towards isolation, self-
affirmation and death) generated the sub-genre of revenge tragedy and
its most celebrated exemplar, Shakespeare's *Hamlet*. Fowler (1982: 114)
identifies this process of specialization as 'the common means of renewal'
in literary art: 'At the level of subgenre, innovation is life. . . . And from
time to time quite fresh subgenres will be invented, enlarging the kind
in new directions altogether'. In his account of the formation of new
genres, as distinct from the development of sub-types within an
established generic form, he points out that many literary inventors are
really mediators of literature from other languages or from the
(sometimes distant) past. Innovation may be the result of assembling a
collection of items from existing generic materials in combinations that
have not occurred before, or transforming a current genre, or reviving one
from beyond the 'generic horizon' of the contemporary cultural scene.
For example, Renaissance comedy, as practised with variations by Lyly,
Shakespeare and Jonson, was a new kind in the immediate historical context of late sixteenth-century English drama, but the playwrights who
created it were able to bring together its distinctive repertoire of features
from an abundance of available resources: comic elements in the native
traditions of religious drama, various forms of popular or courtly entertainment, and motifs from narrative romance, as well as the Latin comedies
of Plautus and Terence that were studied as texts in grammar schools.
Or to take another instance, the kind of verse satire introduced by Donne
and Marston and other poets in the 1590s was quite unlike the types of

satire inherited from the Middle Ages, but its form and style, and some aspects of its content, were deliberately derived from the work of the Roman satirist, Juvenal, who flourished during the reign of Nero. In such cases, Fowler (1982: 157) argues, 'an impression of novelty may result, for the most conscious imitation is often apprehended as originality'.

In such cases, too, to take up your point about the *reception* of a radical work of art, its author will often feel the need to prepare contemporary readers for any excursions that it makes into unfamiliar territory or for generic transformations that might initially be too disorientating or too disruptive of currently accepted norms. In the field of Renaissance comedy, Jonson went to extraordinary lengths in prologues, inductions and epilogues, and even in epistles and critical dialogues appended to the printed texts of his plays, to inform his audiences and his readers of the nature of his latest experiment (often based on reviving or adapting classical precedents), so that they could approach it with the appropriate expectations. Henry Fielding similarly felt the need to introduce *Joseph Andrews* (1742) to the eighteenth-century reader in a critical preface. Explaining that 'this kind of Writing' had not been 'hitherto attempted in our Language' and that 'the mere *English* Reader . . . may consequently expect a kind of Entertainment, not to be found, nor which was even intended, in the following Pages', he defined the relation of this new form of prose fiction to the familiar genres of romance and epic and carefully distinguished between his comic art and 'Writings of the Burlesque kind, which this is not intended to be' (Fielding 1967: 3–4).

Fowler (1982: 168) acknowledges that literature 'may take occasional leaps of generic originality', but even what looks like a genuinely radical departure from existing or previous forms often has behind it experimental predecessors which have slipped into obscurity. Samuel Beckett's *Waiting for Godot* (1952), which so baffled its earliest audiences, has slowly been assimilated as its own conventions – or its characteristic subversions of established dramatic methods – have become part of the literary landscape of the later twentieth century. At the same time, scholars have been gradually uncovering its lines of connection with certain features of Irish drama earlier in the century, which were not apparent to Beckett's first audiences and critics. As a final word on this question of the reception of a radical work of art, let me quote Fowler's (1982: 168–9) view that an extreme case of generic innovation, such as James Joyce's *Finnegans Wake* (1939), may continue to meet strong reader resistance 'until more dilute imitations provide the missing generic context *ex post facto*'.

NW: Johnson's 1765 comment, that Shakespeare's plays were 'compositions of a distinct kind' (quoted on p. 106), seems to challenge some of Frye's working principles. A genre awareness is essential in helping to formulate an approach to a work (you argue persuasively in support of an awareness of forms and their interpretative validity), but it might evade a general value judgement as to whether the design of a work has been well executed, that is, we are helped analytically but may find it difficult to judge the value of what we are reading or seeing. How would you guard against the 'toolkit' approach to analysis?

RW: Like all the tools available for literary analysis and interpretation, the approach through genre may, of course, be applied mechanically. Value judgements – on whether a design has been well executed or indeed on the worth of the insights embodied in or generated by that design – depend upon the aesthetic and moral sensibility, the political attitudes and the breadth of experience (of life and literature) of the reader, not on the mere intellectual analysis of formal or rhetorical features. I agree with Fowler, however, that the first task for the conscientious reader (what he calls 'construction') is accurate observation of the characteristics of the text itself and that interpretation should be based on as full an understanding as possible of what its various features (words, conventions, allusions, structural principles) would have signified to an audience or reader at the time it was produced. Only then is the critic in a position to move beyond interpretation to assessment of value.

Modern genre criticism does not itself assert an evaluative function, which I take is the thrust of your reference to Johnson's remark. A work is no longer (as in some neoclassical criticism) judged according to its conformity to an ideal generic form. Johnson himself recognized that Shakespeare's mixing of features from different genres was an artistic response to pressure from the diversity of human experience, which does not always maintain a rigid separation of seriousness and triviality, gravity and mirth. In so far as a literary genre constitutes what Colie calls a 'fix' upon the world – that is, offers a particular perspective upon life – then it is bound to be selective, to offer only a partial reflection of the totality of human experience. Johnson acknowledged this and saw the range of perspectives made available in a single play as one of the distinctive characteristics of Shakespeare's drama – his 'distinct kind'. One might argue that the complexity of the vision made available by the combination of features from history play, tragedy and comedy in *Antony and Cleopatra* – and the creative tensions that such a combination sets up – affords a possible basis for evaluation. Frye himself tends to regard the generic *forms* (the plot structures or what he terms *mythoi*) of tragedy and comedy as generically exclusive, but he recognizes that much of 'our sense of the subtlety of great literature' (an evaluative principle?) comes from the complicating simultaneous presence of some or all of the five *modes* of his system, that range from myth and romance to satire and irony. He also suggests that, although there is a tendency for each historical period to hold certain modes and genres in greater esteem than others (both in its own literary productions and in its reading of past literature), 'no set of critical standards derived from only one mode can ever assimilate the whole truth about poetry' (Frye 1957: 62). And he issues a timely reminder, for a culture in which the vexed issue of value judgements is clouded by competing ideologies, that 'the two essential facts about a work of art, that it is contemporary with its own time and that it is contemporary with ours, are not opposed but complementary facts' (Frye 1957: 51).

NW: On p. 97, you quote Scholes's plea for an education in 'the grammar of literary forms'. How would you attempt to carry out such a programme in your teaching?

RW: In teaching courses on Elizabethan and Jacobean drama and Renaissance lyric poetry, I attempt to demonstrate to students how a generic repertoire can be assembled, extended and transformed during a period of intensive literary development. We look, for example, at formal, rhetorical and substantive features of the Petrarchan amatory sonnet as practised by such poets as Sidney, Daniel, Drayton and Lady Mary Wroth, the extension and subversion of the genre in the love poetry of John Donne, and later developments through to its deconstruction in the highly allusive and sophisticated lyrics of Andrew Marvell and its adaptation to the theme of friendship among women in the Commonwealth lyrics of Katherine Philips. Similarly, beginning with comedies of the late 1590s such as Dekker's *The Shoemaker's Holiday* (1599) and Jonson's *Every Man in His Humour* (1598), we follow the way in which common features of structure (such as the parallel of romantic and economic/satiric plots, the exposure of folly, the concluding feast or ceremony of reconciliation), common character types (the jealous husband, the reformed prodigal, the witty servant), and common dramatic devices (disguise, soliloquy, the pretence of wealth) are repeated, developed, transgressed and undermined for a variety of celebratory and satiric purposes in such later comedies as *A Trick to Catch the Old One* (1605), *Volpone* (1605), *Bartholomew Fair* (1614), *A Chaste Maid in Cheapside* (1613), and *A New Way to Pay Old Debts* (1625). In this kind of course, there is an emphasis on both the genre awareness of the writers in their production of new texts (prologues and epilogues can be very useful here) and the way in which reader/audience response is enhanced by a growing familiarity with the generic materials that are being exploited in individual examples.

I should add that the generic approach is by no means the only item in the critical toolkit that I encourage students to use, although – as is evident in the foregoing discussion and essay – I regard it as an indispensable tool in the initial stage of 'construction' in the process of coming to terms with an unfamiliar text. To quote Fowler (1982: 113) for a last time: 'Getting to know old literature is very largely a matter of learning the subgenres'.

Endpiece

NIGEL WOOD

Where did Shakespeare's Rome or Alexandria exist? Plutarch might be a likely candidate – or rather Sir Thomas North's translation – but this merely defers the answer, for *why* turn to his account of the lives of the noble Romans and Grecians, and why then? Part of that proof of existence might now be understood in terms of the cultural needs of Elizabethan/Jacobean England: what contemporary debates determined just why the classical past should have been dramatic material? One matter we can be sure about in this regard concerns the degree of accuracy at which the Elizabethan stage aimed when turning to Roman thoughts. Was Shakespeare mistaken when, in *Julius Caesar*, he has Brutus turn down a page (IV.iii.273–4) or has a clock strike (II.i.191) or, in *Coriolanus*, name Roman citizens Hob and Dick (II.iii.112)? In the famous Henry Peacham drawing of a performance of *Titus Andronicus*, while Titus holds a spear and sports Roman armour and a laurel crown, the listening extras wear recognizable Elizabethan dress (described in Eugene M. Waith's Introduction to his edition (Waith 1984: 21; see also Merchant 1957).

What, therefore, do we now do when we do *not* put our Shakespeare productions in modern dress? Archaeology is not simply some disinterested reconstruction of the past. It may aim at that, and our understanding of the glory that was Rome benefits thereby, but, like the placing of the Elgin Marbles in the British Museum, it is a work also of appropriation. The past may be preserved by a more advanced technology, and have fallen to dust if not maintained by it, but it then existed in carefully altered circumstances. This collection analyses the degree to which 'altered circumstances' effectively contribute to the play's changes of meaning. Since its likely first performances at the Globe in 1608 (and possibly, even earlier at the more intimate Blackfriars Theatre) *Antony and Cleopatra* has raised expectations of magnificent staging, yet at the same time its construction has made that possibility something that has had to be engrafted on to it. A common casualty is the Clown in Act V, scene ii, and several of the apparently interleaved scenes that do not inform us of the progress of the central love affair, such as Ventidius and Sillius in Act III, scene i. Increasingly in the nineteenth century, the staging took account of this rather liberal plotting. Scenic theatre demanded that as exact as possible Egyptian furnishings were made or discovered, rather than a reliance on verbal suggestion. Kemble's production at the new Theatre Royal at Covent Garden (1808) replaced the Clown and Pompey with some additions from the more 'heroic' *All for Love* by John Dryden (1677) and a marvellous sea fight for Act III and the closing grandeur of a protracted funeral procession (see Neill 1994: 28–30). Although with never quite the same hubris as Kemble's work, William Macready rendered the play as a non-political and even lyrical experience in 1833, and F.B. Chatterton consulted the newly opened antiquities from the British Museum for his production at Drury Lane in 1873, including the substitution of Enobarbus's description of Antony's first meeting with Cleopatra (II.ii.197–225) by an actual barge with a 'strange invisible perfume' (II.ii.219). The play has become a main-stage spectacle, more by virtue of the opportunities it affords than its purely textual signs.

Without convenient excisions, on the other hand, the Folio text gives us just as much information about how forced and consciously deployed this Alexandrian magic could be, from Philo's acerbic commentary in Act I, scene i, and Enobarbus's interjections in Act II, scene ii, to Antony's botched suicide and Cleopatra's stage-managed death. The play has seemed to invite pruning, and when Dryden adapted it for Restoration tastes this did not only mean in its formal construction. Dryden portrays Octavia's departure from Antony as due to her own wishes to help render the lovers less fixated, and he also does without the multiple plotting that characterized Shakespeare's play. In the interests of plausibility, he gives us a confrontation between Octavia and Cleopatra in Act III, which, he confesses in his Preface, is satirical, but still 'within the bounds of modesty' (Dryden 1975, 11).

The story of the lovers was presented so often in the period that Shakespeare's text gets amalgamated and used for new ends, with the result that its shock values can be underestimated. In Thomas May's

The Tragedy of Cleopatra, Queen of Egypt (1626), for example, strict classicism kept Antony's death of off-stage. Sir Charles Sedley's *Antony and Cleopatra* (1677) begins after the battle of Actium, and, like Dryden's version, obeys the Unity of Time with some remarkable regularity. Nearer to Shakespeare's own writing context, the Countess of Pembroke's *Antonie* (1592) and Samuel Daniel's *Cleopatra* were closet productions with a cast considerably reduced when compared with Shakespeare's version. As with Dryden, the action is wholly centred on Alexandria.

The eighteenth century, indeed, rarely saw the original Shakespearian version. Even when claiming to be returning to the Bard in his 1759 production, David Garrick reduced the number of scenes from a possible 42 to just 27. As Samuel Johnson believed in his edition of 1765, perhaps this was due to the prevailing perception that History organized the account, and not Art, as the action appeared 'without any art of connection or care of disposition' (Johnson 1986: 298). Such irregularity bothered the Romantic commentators much less, yet the refusal to grant the lovers unquestioned tragic status was more of a problem. As if the plot had grown too big for its frame, Hazlitt, for example, noted the power of noble characterization that overwhelmed any signs of moral distaste or formal perfection (in his *Characters of Shakespeare's Plays* 1817): 'Shakespear's genius has spread over the whole play a richness like the overflowing of the Nile' (Bate 1992: 269; see also Bate's (1989: 187–9) comments on Hazlitt's perception of Shakespeare's 'associative imagination').

This volume can hardly claim to have provided us with definitive information as to why Shakespeare experimented as he did with the already well-known plot. It can, however, point to areas of the play that engage with current theoretical interests and also how such interests help illuminate and question our inherited approach to it. If Alexandria now exists (textually, in the play), it must do so in our power to find analogues for it – here and now.

Notes

Introduction

1 This crux in interpretation only begins to be questioned in the early nineteenth century, with William Hazlitt's passages on Shakespeare's boundless empathy in his *The Characters of Shakespeare's Plays* (1817):

> This is a very noble play. . . . [It is] the finest of his historical plays, that is, of those in which he made poetry the organ of history, and assumed a certain tone of character and sentiment, in conformity to known facts, instead of trusting to his observations of general nature or to the unlimited indulgence of his own fancy.
>
> (Bate 1992: 265)

2 There were intermediary Aristotelian influences on the plot. Mary, Countess of Pembroke's adaptation of Robert Garnier's *Marc Antoine*, *Antonius* (1592) and Samuel Daniel's *Tragedie of Cleopatra* (1594) were both possible sources for the latter stages of the play. *Antonius* portrays Cleopatra as a much nobler individual (see Bullough 1957–75, 5: 358–406), whereas the Daniel account deploys a Chorus to keep the play's construction tight (see Bullough 1957–75, 5: 406–49).

3 Daniel's *Tragedie* has no closing view of Caesar in triumph. The Chorus and a Nuntius (Messenger) report on her suicide, and the closing words of the Chorus point to an unequivocal tragic effect: the 'eternall Court/ Of Providence and Right' limits pride and with 'greatnesse' mars 'greatnesse' (Bullough 1957–75, 5: 449). Cinthio's *Cleopatra* (1583) similarly has a Chorus wrap the action up, warning of the snares of Fortune (Bullough 1957–75, 5: 357), but *Antonius* has Cleopatra speak the last words – from

the heart: 'That in this office weake my limmes may growe,/Fainting on you, and forth my soule may flow' (Bullough 1957–75, 5: 406). It is tempting to regard Octavius as Shakespeare's attempt to substitute a worldly Historical influence for the Gods.

4 Note the Soothsayer's appearance in Act I, scene II: 'In nature's infinite book of secrecy/A little I can read' (10–11), and his prognostication of doom for Alexandria, and Enobarbus's growing soothsaying powers (see Act III, scene xiii).

5 See in this regard both Dollimore (1984: 83–108), for the disintegration of Providentialist belief; and Hamilton (1992: 111–27), for the dissensions within Protestant ranks on obedience.

1 Girard's Doubles and Antony and Cleopatra

1 Lacoue-Labarthe's essay is excerpted and translated from Lacoue-Labarthe's 'Typographie' in Mimésis des articulations (Lacoue-Labarthe 1975). Lacoue-Labarthe is responding to both Violence and the Sacred and 'Système du délire', which is Girard's (1972) review of L'Anti-Oedipe by Gilles Deleuze and Felix Guattari.

2 William Johnsen, 'Myth, Ritual, and Literature after Girard', in Natoli (1989: 121) urges a closer coordination of feminist theory with Girard, and suggests (Natoli 1989: 146, note 10) what a 'real dialogue' between Girardian and feminist theory might be.

3 In 'Analysis Terminable and Interminable' Freud (1953–74, 23: 250–51) defines Adler's term 'masculine protest' as the male's relentless 'struggle against his passive or feminine attitude to another male'. Freud registers his preference for the term, 'repudiation of femininity', over the term 'masculine protest'.

4 For a full discussion of the mythological self-fashioning engaged in by the lovers, see Adelman (1973: 68–102).

5 Watson (1978: 409–14) observes that the obvious sources for Shakespeare's depiction of Cleopatra's suicide do not refer to the asp (or asps) at her breast, but that Shakespeare could have found such a reference in Nashe and in Peele and also in Cooper's Thesaurus (1587). See also Bevington (1990: 255, note 303); and Farnham (1956: facing 112).

2 Representing Cleopatra in the Post-colonial Moment

1 On humanism and the exotic, see Dympna Callaghan, 'Re-reading The Tragedie of Mariam, Faire Queen of Jewry', in Hendricks and Parker (1993). On the formation of national identity in early modern drama, see Rackin (1991). On the politics of representing Elizabeth 1, see Tennenhouse (1986: esp. 102–5), Montrose (1983) and Jankowski (1992: Chapter 6).

2 M.R. Ridley, editor of the Arden Antony and Cleopatra, for example,

describes Cleopatra as a 'professional courtesan' (Ridley 1965: xivi).
3 Alloula (1987) demonstrates that even when the real bodies of colonized women were used in postcards the French colonizers sent back to France, their depiction in semi-naked, sexually alluring poses, was entirely one of sexual fantasy (Alloula 1987: 105–24).

3 Reading *Antony and Cleopatra* through Irigaray's *Speculum*

1 The first section of *Speculum* is devoted to a critical dialogue with Freud's lecture on 'Femininity', published in *New Lectures in Psychoanalysis* (Freud 1953–74, 22: 112–35). The third section makes use of the same technique to address Plato's idea of the cave or 'Hysteria' from *Republic*, VII (Plato 1993).
2 The word that Freud used in his original text was 'ich', the ordinary everyday German for 'I'. It was Strachey, his translator, who chose to use the Latin word 'ego', so claiming a place for psychoanalysis within the tradition of Rome.
3 Freud (1953–74, 19: 143–4) declared that little girls were humiliated to find they had no penis, and from this his influential theory of penis envy was derived. Irigaray (1985a: 59–62) develops her own account of why girls and women know they are disadvantaged when they see that no one is going to mistake their body for a man's.
4 Irigaray uses a lot of puns: here she is playing on the Greek prefix *homo* (= the same) and the French *homme* (= man) to produce a provocative term that also carries a trace of reference to same-sex eroticism.

5 . . . it was a wonderful example to the soldiers to see Antonius, that was brought up in all fineness and superfluity, so easily to drink puddle water and to eate wild fruits and rootes: and moreover it is reported, that even as they passed the Alpes, they did eate the barcks of tres. And . . . such beasts as never man tasted of their flesh before.
(Spencer 1964: 191–2)

The war referred to here is that of Mutina (Modena) of 43 BC, where Antony was defeated by the Roman Senate.
6 Freud argued, notably in *The Interpretation of Dreams*, (1900) and his 1915 paper on 'The Unconscious' that the unconscious is timeless. Psychoanalysts disagree about many things but not, apparently, on this point.

4 *Antony and Cleopatra* and Genre Criticism

1 Hernadi (1972: 1) considers that 'the prevailing generic concepts of a period often form the literary horizon beyond which no contemporary reader is likely to see'.
2 Northrop Frye himself has published several books on Shakespeare, most notably *A Natural Perspective: The Development of Shakespearean Comedy*

and Romance (1965), *Fools of Time: Studies in Shakespearean Tragedy* (1967), and *The Myth of Deliverance: Reflections on Shakespeare's Problem Comedies* (1983). Other studies which have taken a similar approach include Barber (1959); Hawkins (1967); Simmons (1969); Snyder (1979); Vincent (1982); and Rozett (1985).

3 See, for example, Danby's (1952: 146) categorical statement that '[t]he tragedy of *Antony and Cleopatra* is, above all, the tragedy of Antony'; and Adelman's (1973: 30) view that 'Antony is the presumptive hero of the play'.

4 See Snyder (1970). It is Friar Francis who counsels Leonato to 'publish it that she is dead indeed' (IV.i.204) after his daughter has been rejected at the altar in *Much Ado About Nothing*; and in *Measure for Measure*, it is in his disguise as a friar that the Duke directs the plot towards its comic resolution.

5 Juliet is similarly dismissive of Romeo's extravagant Petrarchanisms in the balcony scene Act II, ii, and Rosalind points out to Orlando that stories of men dying for love 'are all lies' (*As You Like It*, IV.i.97).

References

Unless otherwise indicated, place of publication is London.

Adelman, Janet (1973) *The Common Liar: An Essay on Antony and Cleopatra*. New Haven, CT.

Alcoff, Linda (1991–2) 'The Problem of Speaking for Others', *Cultural Critique*, 20: 5–32.

Alloula, Malek (1987) *The Colonial Harem*, trans. Myrna Godzich and Wlad Godzich. Manchester.

Aristotle (1965) *Aristotle, Horace, Longinus: Classical Literary Criticism*, trans. T.S. Dorsch. Harmondsworth.

Aristotle (1968) *Aristotle's Poetics: A Translation and Commentary for Students of Literature*, trans. Leon Golden, commentary by O.B. Hardison, Jnr. Englewood Cliffs, NJ.

Armstrong, Isobel (ed.) (1992) *New Feminist Discourses: Critical Essays on Theory and Texts*.

Ashcroft, Bill, Griffiths, Gareth and Tiffin, Helen (eds) (1989) *The Empire Writes Back: Theory and Practice in Post-colonial Literatures*.

Attridge, Derek, Bennington, Geoff and Young, Robert (eds) (1987) *Post-Structuralism and the Question of History*. Cambridge.

Barber, C. L. (1959) *Shakespeare's Festive Comedy*. Princeton, NJ.

Bate, Jonathan (1989) *Shakespearean Constitutions: Politics, Theatre, Criticism 1730–1830*. Oxford.

Bate, Jonathan (ed.) (1992) *The Romantics on Shakespeare*. Harmondsworth.

Berry, Philippa (1989) *Of Chastity and Power: Elizabethan Literature and the Unmarried Queen*.

Bevington, David (1990) Introduction, in Bevington (ed.) *Antony and Cleopatra* (Shakespeare). Cambridge.

Bradley, A.C. (1905) *Shakespearean Tragedy*.

Bradley, A.C. (1909) *Oxford Lectures on Poetry*.

Brantlinger, Patrick (1990) *Crusoe's Footprints: Cultural Studies in Britain and America*.

Brennan, Teresa (1992) *The Interpretation of the Flesh: Freud and Femininity*.

Brodwin, Leonora Leet (1972) *Elizabethan Love Tragedy: 1587–1625*.

Bullough, Geoffrey (1957–75) *Narrative and Dramatic Sources of Shakespeare*, 8 vols.

Callaghan, Dympna (1989) *Woman and Gender in Renaissance Tragedy*. Brighton.

Coleridge, Samuel Taylor (1907) *Coleridge's Essays and Lectures on Shakespeare*.

Colie, Rosalie (1973) *The Resources of Kind: Genre-Theory in the Renaissance*. Berkeley, CA.

Colie, Rosalie (1974) *Shakespeare's Living Art*. Princeton, NJ.

Croce, Benedetto (1968) *Aesthetic*, trans. Douglas Ainslie. New York.

Culler, Jonathan (1975) *Structuralist Poetics: Structuralism, Linguistics and the Study of Literature*.

Culler, Jonathan (1981) *In Pursuit of Signs: Semiotics, Literature, Deconstruction*. Ithaca, NY.

Danby, John F. (1952) *Poets on Fortune's Hill*.

Davies, H. Neville (1985) 'Jacobean 'Antony and Cleopatra', *Shakespeare Studies*, 7: 123–58.

Derrida, Jacques (1976) *Of Grammatology*, trans. Gayatri Chakravorty Spivak. Baltimore, MD.

Derrida, Jacques (1982) *Dissemination*, trans. Barbara Johnson. Chicago.

Dollimore, Jonathan (1984) *Radical Tragedy: Religion, Ideology and Power in the Drama of Shakespeare and His Contemporaries*. Hemel Hempstead.

Dryden, John (1975) *All for Love*, ed. N.J. Andrew.

Farnham, Willard (1956) *The Medieval Heritage of Elizabethan Tragedy*. New York (1st. ed., 1936).

Fergusson, Francis (1961) 'Introduction', in *Aristotle's Poetics*, trans. S.H. Butcher. New York.

Fielding, Henry (1967) *Joseph Andrews*, ed. Martin C. Battestin. Oxford.

Fineman, Joel (1977) 'Fratricide and Cuckoldry: Shakespeare's Doubles', *Psychoanalytic Review*, 64: 409–53.

Fowler, Alastair (1982) *Kinds of Literature: An Introduction to the Theory of Genres and Modes*. Oxford.

Freud, Sigmund (1953–74) *The Standard Edition of the Complete Psychological Works*, ed. J. Strachey, 24 vols.

Frye, Northrop (1957) *Anatomy of Criticism: Four Essays*. New York.

Frye, Northrop (1965) *A Natural Perspective: The Development of Shakespearean Comedy*. San Diego, CA.

Frye, Northrop (1967) *Fools of Time: Studies in Shakespearean Tragedy*. Toronto.

Frye, Northrop (1983) *The Myth of Deliverance: Reflections on Shakespeare's Problem Comedies*. Toronto.

Girard, René (1965) *Deceit, Desire and the Novel*, trans. Yvonne Fecerro. Baltimore, MD.

Girard, René (1972) 'Système du délire', *Critique*, 28: 957–96.

Girard, René (1973) 'Lévi-Strauss, Frye, Derrida and Shakespearean Criticism', *Diacritics*, 3: 34–8.

Girard, René (1977a) *Violence and the Sacred*, trans. Patrick Gregory. Baltimore, MD.

Girard, René (1977b) *Des Choses Cachées Depuis la Fondation du Monde* (with Jean-Michel Oughourlian and Guy Lefort). Paris.

Girard, René (1978a) 'Interview', *Diacritics*, 8: 31–54.

Girard, René (1978b) '*To Double Business Bound': Essays on Literature, Mimesis, and Anthropology*. Baltimore. MD.

Girard, René (1986) *The Scapegoat*, trans. Yvonne Feccero. Baltimore, MD.

Girard, René (1989) 'Love Delights in Praises: A Reading of *Two Gentlemen of Verona*', *Philosophy and Literature*, 13: 231–47.

Girard, René (1991) *A Theater of Envy*. New York.

Gramsci, Antonio (1971) *Selections From the Prison Notebooks*, ed. Quintin Hoare and Geoffrey Nowell Smith.

Greville, Fulke (1870) *The Works in Verse and Prose Complete of the Rt. Hon. Fulke Greville*, ed. Rev. Alexander B. Grosart. 4 vols. Blackburn.

Guha, Ranajit (1983a) *Elementary Aspects of Peasant Insurgency in Colonial India*. Delhi.

Guha, Ranajit (ed.) (1983b) *Subaltern Studies: Writings on South Asian History and Society*, volume II. Delhi.

Guha, Ranajit (ed.) (1987) *Subaltern Studies: Writings on South Asian History and Society*, volume V. Delhi.

Hamer, Mary (1993) *Signs of Cleopatra: History, Politics, Representation*.

Hamilton, Donna B. (1992) *Shakespeare and the Politics of Protestant England*. New York.

Harris, Duncan S. (1977) ' "Again for Cydnus": The Dramaturgical Resolution of *Antony and Cleopatra*', *Studies in English Literature*, 17: 219–31.

Hawkins, Sherman (1967) 'The Two Worlds of Shakespearean Comedy', *Shakespeare Studies*, 3: 62–80.

Heidegger, Martin (1961) *Introduction to Metaphysics*. New York.

Hendricks, Margo and Parker, Patricia (eds) (1993) *Women, Race, and Writing in the Renaissance*. London.

Hernadi, Paul (1972) *Beyond Genre: New Directions in Literary Classification*. Ithaca, NY.

Hirsch, E.D. (1967) *Validity in Interpretation*. New Haven, CT.

Hirsch, E.D. (1976) *The Aims of Interpretation*. Chicago, IL.

Hughes-Hallett, Lucy (1990) *Cleopatra: Histories, Dreams, and Distortions*.

Irigaray, Luce (1985a) *Speculum of the Other Woman*, trans. Gillian C. Gill. Ithaca, NY.

Irigaray, Luce (1985b) *This Sex Which Is Not One*. trans. Catherine Porter. Ithaca, NY.

Irigaray, Luce (1991) *The Irigaray Reader*, ed. Margaret Whitford. Oxford.

Jankowski, Theodore A. (1992) *Women in Power in The Early Modern Drama*. Urbana, IL.

Jauss, Hans Robert (1970) 'Literary History as a Challenge to Literary Theory', trans. Elizabeth Benzinger, *New Literary History*, 2: 7–37.

Johnson, Samuel (1986) *Selections From Johnson on Shakespeare*, ed. Bertrand H. Bronson, with Jean O'Meara. New Haven, CT.

Jones, Emrys (1971) *Scenic Form in Shakespeare*. Oxford.

Juilland, Alphonse (ed.) (1986) *To Honor René Girard*. Stanford, CA.

Kennedy, George A. (ed.) (1989) *Classical Criticism* (Vol. 1 of the Cambridge History of Literary Criticism). Cambridge.

Lacoue-Labarthe, Philippe (1975) *Mimésis des articulations*. Paris.

Lacoue-Labarthe, Philippe (1978) 'Mimesis and Truth'. *Diacritics*, 8: 10–23.

Livingston, Paisley (1992) *Models of Desire: René Girard and the Psychology of Mimesis*. Baltimore, MD.

McRobbie, Angela (1985) 'Strategies of Vigilance. An Interview with Gayatri Chakravorti Spivak', *Block*, 10: 1–7.

Marx, Karl (1977) *Selected Writings*, ed. David McLellan. Oxford.

Mason, H.A. (1970) *Shakespeare's Tragedies of Love*.

Merchant, W.M. (1957) 'Classical costumes in Shakespearian Productions', *Shakespeare Survey*, 10: 71–6.

Miola, Robert S. (1983) *Shakespeare's Rome*. Cambridge.

Mitchell, Juliet and Rose, Jacqueline (eds) (1982) *Feminine Sexuality*. New York.

Moi, Toril (1985) *Sexual/Textual Politics: Feminist Literary Theory*.

Montrose, Louis (1983) 'Shaping Fantasies: Figurations of Gender and Power in Elizabethan Culture', *Representations*, 1: 61–94.

Morris, Helen (1969) 'Queen Elizabeth I 'shadowed' in Cleopatra', *Huntingdon Library Quarterly*, 32: 271–8.

Natoli, Joseph (ed.) (1989) *Literary Theory's Future(s)*. Urbana, IL.

Neill, Michael (1994) Introduction, in Neill (ed.), *Anthony and Cleopatra*. Oxford.

Nelson, Cary and Grossberg, Lawrence (eds) (1988) *Marxism and the Interpretation of Culture*. Basingstoke.

Nicoll, Allardyce (1960–61) ' "Tragical-Comical-Historical-Pastoral": Elizabethan Dramatic Nomenclature', *Bulletin of the John Rylands Library, Manchester*, 43: 70–87.

Orgel, Stephen (1979) 'Shakespeare and the Kinds of Drama', *Critical Inquiry*, 6: 107–23.

Parker, R.B. (1994) Introduction, in Parker (ed.), *Coriolanus*. Oxford.

Rackin, Phyllis (1972) 'Shakespeare's Boy Cleopatra, the Decorum of Nature and the Golden World of Poetry', *Publications of the Modern Language Association of America*, 87: 201–11.

Rackin, Phyllis (1991) *Stages of History*. Ithaca, NY.

Reinhart, Keith (1972) 'Shakespeare's Cleopatra and England's Elizabeth', *Shakespeare Quarterly*, 23: 81–6.

Ridley, M.R. (ed.) (1965) *Antony and Cleopatra*.

Rozett, Martha Tuck (1985) 'The Comic Structures of Tragic Endings: The Suicide Scenes in *Romeo and Juliet* and *Antony and Cleopatra*', *Shakespeare Quarterly*, 36: 152–64.

Said, Edward (1978) *Orientalism: Western Conceptions of the Orient.*

Said, Edward (1984) *The World, the Text and the Critic.*

Schanzer, Ernest (1963) *The Problem Plays of Shakespeare.*

Scholes, Robert (1974) *Structuralism in Literature: An Introduction.* New Haven, CT.

Sidney, Sir Philip (1973) *A Defence of Poetry*, ed. J.A. Van Dorsten. Oxford.

Simmons, J.L. (1969) 'The Comic Pattern and Vision in *Antony and Cleopatra*', *English Literary History*, 36: 493–510.

Singh, Jyotsna (1989) 'Renaissance Antitheatricality, Antifeminism, and Shakespeare's *Antony and Cleopatra*', *Renaissance Drama*, 20: 99–127.

Snyder, Susan (1970) '*Romeo and Juliet*: Comedy into Tragedy', *Essays in Criticism*, 20: 391–402.

Snyder, Susan (1979) *The Comic Matrix of Shakespeare's Tragedies.* Princeton, NJ.

Spencer, T.J.B. (ed.) (1964) *Shakespeare's Plutarch.* Harmondsworth.

Spivak, Gayatri Chakravorty (1988) *In Other Worlds: Essays in Cultural Politics.* New York.

Spivak, Gayatri Chakravorty (1990) *The Post-colonial Critic*, ed. Sarah Harasym. New York.

Stauffer, Donald A. (1949) *Shakespeare's World of Images.* New York.

Taylor, Gary (1989) *Reinventing Shakespeare: A Cultural History from the Restoration to the Present.*

Tennenhouse, Leonard (1986) *Power on Display: The Politics of Shakespeare's Genres.*

Thomas, Brook (1991) *The New Historicism and Other Old-fashioned Topics.* Princeton, NJ.

Traversi, Derek (1963) *Shakespeare: The Roman Plays.*

Vincent, Barbara C. (1982) 'Shakespeare's *Antony and Cleopatra* and the Rise of Comedy', *English Literary Renaissance*, 12: 53–86.

Viswanathan, Gauri (1989) *Masks of Conquest: Literary Study and the British Rule in India.* New York.

Waith, Eugene M. (1984) Introduction, in Waith (ed.) *Titus Andronicus.* Oxford.

Watson, G. (1978) 'The death of Cleopatra', *Notes and Queries*, 25: 409–14.

Whitaker, Virgil K. (1965) *The Mirror up to Nature: The Technique of Shakespeare's Tragedies.* San Marino, CA.

Whitford, Margaret (1991) *Luce Irigaray: Philosophy in the Feminine.*

Williams, Raymond (1977) *Marxism and Literature.* Oxford.

Woolf, Virginia (1992) *A Room of One's Own and Three Guineas*, ed. Morag Shiach. Oxford.

Yachnin, Paul (1993) 'Shakespeare's politics of loyalty: sovereignty and subjectivity in *Antony and Cleopatra*', *Studies in English Literature*, 33: 343–63.

Further Reading

1 Girard's Doubles and *Antony and Cleopatra*

Diacritics, 8 (Spring 1978).
This issue of *Diacritics* is devoted to René Girard and to various responses to his theory.

René Girard, *A Theater of Envy* (New York, 1991).
In this volume, Girard has collected and revised his many essays on selected works in the Shakespearian canon: *The Two Gentlemen of Verona*, *The Rape of Lucrece*, *A Midsummer Night's Dream*, *Much Ado About Nothing*, *As You Like It*, *Twelfth Night*, *Troilus and Cressida*, *Timon of Athens*, *Julius Caesar*, *The Merchant of Venice*, *Hamlet*, *Othello*, the *Sonnets*, *The Winter's Tale* and *The Tempest*.

René Girard, *Deceit, Desire, and the Novel*, trans. Yvonne Feccero (Baltimore, MD, 1965).
Primarily a study of the nineteenth-century novel, this work is Girard's first full-length account of mimetic, 'triangular' desire and rivalry.

René Girard, *'To Double Business Bound': Essays on Literature, Mimesis, and Anthropology* (Baltimore, MD 1978).
Exploring mimetic desire and rivalry from both a literary and an anthropological perspective, this work provides the best overall perspective of Girard's theory.

René Girard, *Violence and the Sacred*, trans. Patrick Gregory (Baltimore, MD, 1972).

Primarily an anthropological study, this work explores the origins of and relationship between violence and sacrifice.

Paisley Livingston, *Models of Desire: René Girard and the Psychology of Mimesis* (Baltimore, MD 1992).
This study attempts a reconstruction of Girard's theory of mimesis and is both an elucidation and a reformulation of Girard's views.

2 Representing Cleopatra in the Post-colonial Moment

Gayatari Spivak, *In Other Worlds* (New York, 1988)
This is the major collection of Spivak's essays. It is probably the most important articulation of the connection between feminism, post-colonialism, post-structuralism and Marxism available.

Malek Alloula, *The Colonial Harem* (Minneapolis, MN, 1986).
This book is a collection of photographs – postcards sent home by the French from Algiers. It reveals the fantasy of the exotic woman. For instance, women whose culture deplored nudity were shown bare-breasted on postcards as if they might be found in such condition by any casual observer on a street in Algiers.

Robert Young, *White Mythologies: Writing History and the West* (London, 1990).
A lucid introduction to the issues of race and imperialism as they relate to the West's understanding of itself.

Fredric Jameson, ' "Third World Literature": A short essay in defence of the term "Third World" ', *New German Critique* (1989).
When it was first published, critics responded that Jameson was miscategorizing and oversimplifying non-Western literature. However, Jameson's point is that capitalism has produced the division between First and Third World, and that to ignore this is to turn a blind eye to the economic conditions in which literature is currently produced.

Margo Hendricks and Pat Parker (eds), *Women, Race and Writing* (London, 1993).
A collection of essays on race and gender in the early modern period with useful expositions of the category of 'race' as well as readings of both canonical and non-canonical texts.

3 Reading *Antony and Cleopatra* through Irigaray's *Speculum*

Carol Gilligan, *In a Different Voice*, 2nd edn (Cambridge, MA, 1993).
The book that revealed that the accounts of human development built up in developmental psychology had been based on all-male samples. In the core

essay Gilligan listens to the language two groups of people used to frame the moral choices they were faced with. She shows how the women's account of their problem was cast in terms that were different from the ones the men chose to explain their situation to themselves.

Elizabeth Harvey, *Ventriloquized Voices*, (London, 1992).
Harvey interrogates the appropriation of the feminine voice by male authors. The result is the 'voice of gender', an almost androgynous ambivalence where a space is opened up between expected stock responses. Harvey is especially valuable in her re-readings of texts as diverse as Donne's verse, Erasmus's *In Praise of Folly*, and Ovid's multivalent protagonists.

Luce Irigaray, *Je, Tu, Nous: Toward a Culture of Difference* (London, 1993).
A very clear introduction to Irigaray's work, written for a more popular audience than *Speculum*. Easy as it is to get through, it rests on a dense and resilient theoretical base, so it is a relatively painless way of learning about the distinctiveness of her thought and seeing how she herself applies it to contemporary problems and conditions. Particularly interesting is the philosophical attention she pays to the placenta and its function.

Patsy Rodenburg, *The Need for Words: Voice and the Text* (London, 1993).
This book, by the Head of Voice at the National Theatre, offers a voice-centred approach to Shakespeare and other texts for performance. It is an invaluable supplement to more academic ones. She shows how you might listen for a speaker's emotional shifts as they are registered by Shakespeare's language and insists on the connection between the voice and the rest of the body.

Margaret Whitford, *Luce Irigaray: Philosophy in the Feminine* (London, 1991).
An extremely clear and well-paced introduction to the body of Irigaray's published work. Whitford is an admirable guide, careful to make sure the reader understands where her own argument is going, probing and elucidating as she moves on. A pleasure in its own right.

4 *Antony and Cleopatra* and Genre Criticism

Rosalie L. Colie, *The Resources of Kind: Genre Theory in the Renaissance* edited by Barbara K. Lewalski (Berkeley, Los Angeles and London, 1973).
A series of four lectures which emphasizes the variety of genres and generic functions in Renaissance literature. Particular attention is given to the genre system as a set of recognized frames for looking at the real world and to the practice of generic experimentation by mixing genres.

Rosalie L. Colie, *Shakespeare's Living Art* (Princeton, NJ, 1974).
A defence of the view that it is only by generic forms and norms that an art exists and is communicated from one imagination and one generation to another. The argument is grounded in the demonstration that questions of

form and convention were of utmost concern to Renaissance writers and that Shakespeare's art in particular was responsive to the problematic nature, rather than the stereotypical force, of literary traditions.

Heather Dubrow, *Genre* (The Critical Idiom, 42) (London and New York, 1982).

A useful introduction to the history of genre criticism from Aristotle to the twentieth century, highlighting the different theoretical views on the nature and function of genres in different periods.

Alastair Fowler, *Kinds of Literature: An Introduction to the Theory of Genres and Modes* (Oxford, 1982).

The most comprehensive account of genre theory as it has been extended and adapted in the context of recent theoretical approaches to the study of language and literature.

Northrop Frye, *A Natural Perspective: The Development of Shakespearean Comedy and Romance* (San Diego, New York and London, 1965); *Fools of Time: Studies in Shakespearean Tragedy* (Toronto, Buffalo and London, 1967); *The Myth of Deliverance: Reflections on Shakespeare's Problem Comedies* (Brighton, 1983).

Three sets of lectures in which the author of *Anatomy of Criticism* explores formal and thematic variations within the generic constraints of three broad categories of Shakespearian drama.

Claudio Guillén, *Literature as System: Essays Towards the Theory of Literary History* (Princeton, NJ, 1971).

An influential contribution to literary theory which argues that the concept of genre occupies a central position in the study of literary history and which develops the fruitful ideas of genre as an invitation to form and of the dialogue between pairs of contrasting genres such as pastoral and satire.

Paul Hernadi, *Beyond Genre: New Directions in Literary Classification* (Ithaca, NY, and London, 1972).

A survey of different modern formulations of genre theory, which argues that for practical purposes generic criticism must abandon the monistic principle of classification for the diverse resources of several systems of coordinates in order to reflect the many respects in which literary works can usefully be classified as similar.

Index

Figures in parentheses after note entries indicate the relevant chapter number.